LIFELINES

GUIDANCE
⇐===== *for* =====⇒
Building Boundaries
Around My Life

MARK EVANS

LifeLines
Copyright © 2019 by Mark Evans
ALL RIGHTS RESERVED

Published by Lifetogether Ministries.

Unless otherwise noted, all Scripture quotes are taken from the HOLY BIBLE, NEW INTERNATIONAL VERSION®. Copyright© 1973, 1978, 1984, and 2011 by Biblica, Inc.® Used by permission. All rights reserved worldwide.

Scripture quotations marked (MSG) are taken from *The Message*. Copyright © 1993, 1994, 1995, 1996, 2000, 2001, 2002 by Eugene Peterson. Used by permission of NavPress Publishing Group.

Scripture quotations marked (TLB) are from The Living Bible. Copyright © 1971by Tyndale House Foundation. Used by permission of Tyndale House Publishers Inc., Carol Stream, Illinois 60188. All rights reserved.

Scriptures marked as "(GNT)" are taken from the Good News Translation - Second Edition © 1992 by American Bible Society. Used by permission.

Scripture quotations are from the ESV® Bible (The Holy Bible, English Standard Version®), copyright © 2001 by Crossway, a publishing ministry of Good News Publishers. Used by permission. All rights reserved.

Scripture taken from the New Century Version®. Copyright © 2005 by Thomas Nelson. Used by permission. All rights reserved.

Scripture taken from the New King James Version®. Copyright © 1982 by Thomas Nelson. Used by permission. All rights reserved.
Scriptures marked KJV are taken from the KING JAMES VERSION (KJV): KING JAMES VERSION, public domain.

Scriptures marked HCSB are taken from the HOLMAN CHRISTIAN STANDARD BIBLE (HCSB): Scripture taken from the HOLMAN CHRISTIAN STANDARD BIBLE, copyright© 1999, 2000, 2002, 2003 by Holman Bible Publishers, Nashville Tennessee. All rights reserved.

The New Testament in Modern English by J.B Phillips copyright © 1960, 1972 J. B. Phillips. Administered by The Archbishops' Council of the Church of England. Used by Permission.

All rights reserved. No part of this publication may be produced, stores in a retrieval system, or transmitted in any form or by any means–electronic, mechanical, photocopy, recording, or otherwise–except for brief quotations in printed reviews, without the prior written permission of the publisher.

Cover and interior design by Krista Joy Johnson.
Written in partnership with Lisa Guest.

ISBN 978-1-950007-36-3 *(hardcover)*

Printed in the United States of America. First printing April 2019.

LIFELINES
are invaluable *for* you...because they *add* value *to* you!

You will discover that every LifeLine you establish will serve as a **guardrail that protects you** and a **guidewire that directs you.**

We all need to be protected at times. We need *protection from other people* who will try to harm us. And we need *protection from ourselves* when we forget how to make healthy decisions.

Those are the times a good guardrail reminds me that we are valuable...valuable to ourselves, to people and to God. That we are worth protecting!

And who doesn't require daily direction? Guidewires that *direct us* make a *statement about who I am*. And *solidify why I am.*

These guidewires you will hold onto help you remember you really have a purpose given to you by God.

They maintain that you are important to yourself, to people and to God. That God put you on the planet to be a part of something that is bigger than yourself.

I am proud to dedicate this book to our grandchildren, Ruthie Jane Reynolds and Brayden Mark Evans.

It is the prayer of my heart that each of them always establish strong LifeLines around their lives...and that they fall in love with Jesus, who is The One LifeLine that will always protect them and direct them.

Mark Evans

TABLE OF CONTENTS

RELATIONSHIPS

① Recognizing Toxic People.. 6
② Another's Toxicity Is Not About You 13
③ Dealing with Toxic People... 20
④ Wisdom for Relationships... 27
⑤ Life-Changing Acceptance 34

The Week in Review 41
Personal Reflection or Group Discussion Questions............................. 42

TIME

① How Are You?.. 45
② Saying No to the Good and Yes to the Best 52
③ A Life Out of Balance.. 59
④ Finding Balance... 66
⑤ Why Are We Pushing So Hard? 73

The Week in Review 80
Personal Reflection or Group Discussion Questions............................. 81

SPIRITIUAL HEALTH

① Which Part of the Rope?.. 84
② Spiritual Solutions for Spiritual Stress................................ 91
③ Keeping Your Spiritual Commitments 98
④ Physical Health, Spiritual Significance 105
⑤ Health of Our Whole Being 112

The Week in Review 119
Personal Reflection or Group Discussion Questions............................ 120

WORK

❶ The Cause and Consequences of Burnout 123
❷ First Aid for Burnout. 130
❸ What Are You Focused On?. 137
❹ Hostile Coworkers. 144
❺ The Burden of Unrealistic Expectations. 151

The Week in Review *158*
Personal Reflection or Group Discussion Questions. *159*

MONEY

❶ Becoming a Giver 162
❷ A Boy's Example 169
❸ If Saving Is a Foreign Language 176
❹ It Will Rain!. 183
❺ Honoring God by Our Giving 190

The Week in Review *197*
Personal Reflection or Group Discussion Questions. *198*

1

RELATIONSHIPS

RECOGNIZING TOXIC PEOPLE

It's true about all our shortcomings: we see more easily in other people the faults, flaws, and foibles that we ourselves are guilty of. We see their legalism, hypocrisy, nitpicking, and guilt-tripping while too often being oblivious to our own. Yet being able to recognize these traits as typical of toxic people can help us avoid toxic relationships.

First, legalism is a sign that a person is toxic. Legalists have long lists of rules and regulations outlining the ways they think things are to be done.

In Luke 11, for instance, Jesus went to a Pharisee's home for lunch. As Jesus approached His place at the table, He walked past the station set up by the Pharisee for ritual hand-washing, a complicated invention of devout Jews. With details dating back five centuries, this ritual had become tradition, and tradition took on the character of law. So the Pharisee noticed that Jesus didn't wash before the meal: "The Pharisee was shocked and somewhat offended when he saw that Jesus didn't wash up for meals" (v. 38 MSG). Legalism is always about rules, not relationships.

That's why legalistic Christians are always getting offended, upset, and mad. They let us know whenever we're not measuring up to their standards. Forever being offended, legalists live in a state of being upset.

Jesus always offended legalists because they could not control Him with their rules. They couldn't manage Him because He had a totally different perspective on life. Life is not about rules and regulations and rituals and policies and performance. It's about love; it's about relationships. Jesus didn't play by their rules, and they didn't like it.

Another indication of toxicity is hypocrisy. Simply put, hypocrisy is not doing what you say you believe in. You push rules onto everybody else but don't keep them yourself.

The word hypocrisy comes from Greek drama and refers to the masks that actors—who had several roles in a given play—would wear to indicate which character they were portraying. Whatever their roles, the actors were always pretending.

The hypocritical Pharisees wanted to pat themselves on the back for what they were doing and impress those who noticed them. The Pharisees, for example, were careful about their tithing, even counting the sprinkles of herbs from their garden, yet they would allow their neighbors to suffer. They failed to love God the way He wants to be loved. A genuine relationship can't be reduced to a list of rules. People who try to build a relationship within their own rules are toxic.

Next, people who love to find fault are toxic. These nitpicking people are judgmental, critical of your actions and your words—which they love to twist. When the Pharisees were trying to get rid of Jesus, they "went out and laid plans to trap him in his words" (Matthew 22:15).

Jesus never put up with this kind of nitpicking. When the Pharisees criticized Him for healing on the Sabbath, Jesus quoted Hosea 6:6—"I desire mercy, not sacrifice." Furthermore, toxic people tend to think in terms of black and white. You're either all bad, or you're all good. In their toxicity, nitpickers offer no grace. Jesus is more concerned about people's well-being than their obsessive focus on keeping the law.

TOXIC PEOPLE LOVE TO MAKE OTHER PEOPLE FEEL GUILTY.

Finally, toxic people love to make other people feel guilty. They're very good at blaming, condemning, shaming, denouncing, and piling on guilt. Toxic people love to use the words should, must, have to, and ought to. Jesus confronted the Pharisees on exactly that matter: "You load people down with burdens they can hardly carry, and you yourselves will not lift one finger to help them" (Luke 11:46).

Implicit in a toxic person's shoulds and oughts is the message, "If you would just change, then things would be great for me, and I would be happy."

You and I are as happy as we choose to be. A person tries to make his or her happiness dependent upon how you act is toxic.

So, among other things, toxic people are legalistic, hypocritical, faultfinding, and guilt tripping. As unhelpful and even damaging as these behaviors are, they are even more destructive when they are done by God's people acting as His representatives. God is more concerned about heart than behavior, about a relationship than rules, and beware of people whose actions suggest the opposite values.

LIFELINE
Beware of people who are legalistic, hypocritical, faultfinding, and guilt-tripping—and of becoming one yourself.

DIGGING DEEPER

LIFELINE
Beware of people who are legalistic, hypocritical, faultfinding, and guilt-tripping—and of becoming one yourself.

"Love the Lord your God with all your heart and with all your soul and with all your mind.' This is the first and greatest commandment. And the second is like it: 'Love your neighbor as yourself.'"
JESUS IN MATTHEW 22:37-39

"Woe to you, teachers of the law and Pharisees, you hypocrites! You are like whitewashed tombs, which look beautiful on the outside but on the inside are full of the bones of the dead and everything unclean. In the same way, on the outside, you appear to people as righteous but on the inside, you are full of hypocrisy and wickedness."
JESUS IN MATTHEW 23:27-28

Do not let any unwholesome talk come out of your mouths, but only what is helpful for building others up according to their needs, that it may benefit those who listen.
EPHESIANS 4:29

Below, write down any ideas prompted by either these verses or the following questions...

What could be the connection between toxicity and self-centeredness?

What is appealing about legalism? What makes a relationship with Jesus more demanding than keeping rules?

Why is hypocrisy antithetical to love?

IN REAL LIFE

Two thousand years ago the apostle James wrote, "Be doers of the word, and not hearers only" (1:22). Reading and understanding the Bible is good, but it's not enough. We also need to put into action what we read. We need to be "doers of the word."

What idea from today's reading seems to be just for you?

What will you do in response to that insight? Be specific.

TALK IT THROUGH

We tend to make prayer more complicated than it needs to be. Prayer is simply having a conversation with God: we listen, and we speak.

LIFELINE
Beware of people who are legalistic, hypocritical, faultfinding, and guilt-tripping—and of becoming one yourself.

Listening
Spend a few minutes simply being quiet. As you consider the ideas in today's reading—including the LifeLine—what thoughts does God bring to mind? You may get a sense that you are to start doing something—or stop doing something. Perhaps you will recognize some changes that might be good to make.

Talking
Speak to God as if He is sitting right next to you—and use the everyday words you would use if you were talking to a friend. Thank God for what He has taught you about people to beware of. Ask Him to help you use what you've learned. One of these may help you get started:

Help me see in myself any of the legalism, hypocrisy, faultfinding, and guilt-tripping that I so easily see in others—and then help me change!

Keep me from crossing the line between being aware of toxic people and judging them.

2
RELATIONSHIPS
ANOTHER'S TOXICITY IS NOT ABOUT YOU

My good friend Greg and I regularly remind each other that he who reveals the problem becomes the problem—in the minds of those whose problem it is!

In my role as a pastor, I often counsel people who are struggling. Many times, the counselee is shocked to hear about what is clearly their problem. Too often counselees refuse to accept responsibility for their part in the problem, and that problem becomes the counselor's fault!

I can't count how many times I've been blamed for people's self-made dysfunction when their problems—their toxicity—is truly not about me at all.

That truth is worth repeating: a toxic person's choice to blame you or shame you is not about you. Toxic people love to blame others for their pain, but it's not about you. It's about them. As I've said, we human beings are as happy as we choose to be. It's easier to blame someone for our unhappiness, but that's crazy.

And maybe you've noticed this. When you get crazy makers around you, their craziness can get you wondering, Am I going crazy? When they flip around your words, you may think, I know they're crazy—but am I crazy too?

Let me assure you that you are not crazy. Their toxic thoughts, words, and behaviors are not about you. When we're dealing with crazymakers, we do well to follow Paul's wise advice in Romans 12:18—"If it is possible, as far as it depends on you, live at peace with everyone."

Did you see the two qualifiers, though? *If* and *as far as it depends on you* are important. When you don't play the role that toxic people want you to play, they are still going to get upset. In fact, with some people, it doesn't matter what you do. They will still be upset. This reaction doesn't have anything to do with you. It has to do with their pain.

In other words, you didn't create their toxic behavior—their fearfulness, bitterness, envy, greed, belittling ways, nagging, or nitpicking. You didn't create any of those emotions or the behaviors they prompt, so you don't have to feel guilty about it. Toxic people might want to blame you, but you are not responsible.

In addition, you can't control anybody else's behavior, whether it's good or bad, healthy or toxic. Another person's behavior is neither your fault nor something you need to try to control. God does not expect you to control it.

Similarly, you can't change another person's behavior. Don't even try. You'll be wasting your time. A person doesn't change until he or she decides to change. You can't change anybody. You can only change yourself. People only change when the fear of change is exceeded by the pain of not changing—and many toxic people have an amazingly high pain tolerance. They are more afraid of change than they are of handling the pain that they create for themselves and everybody else. And they live in misery.

> **ANOTHER PERSON'S BEHAVIOR IS NEITHER YOUR FAULT NOR SOMETHING YOU NEED TO TRY TO CONTROL.**

So you didn't create another person's toxic behavior, you can't control it, and you're not going to change it. Another person's behavior is not about you.

It's not rocket science! You don't have to show up where the toxic people are. When Jesus called out the Pharisees for their hypocrisy, the disciples asked Him, "Do You realize You offended the Pharisees by what You just said?" Jesus' answer was simple: "Ignore them. They are blind guides leading the blind" (Matthew 15:12, 14 NLT).

If a toxic somebody keeps calling you, emailing you, or showing up at Starbuck's every time you're there, change your number, get a spam blocker, or choose a new Starbuck's. It's not that hard.

LIFELINE
A person's toxicity is not about you.
Pull back. Disconnect. Let the toxic people go.

DIGGING DEEPER

LIFELINE
A person's toxicity is not about you.
Pull back. Disconnect. Let the toxic people go.

*I do not sit with the deceitful,
nor do I associate with hypocrites.*

*I abhor the assembly of evildoers
and refuse to sit with the wicked.*
PSALM 26:4-5

The righteous choose their friends carefully.
PROVERBS 12:26

"Why do you look at the speck of sawdust in your brother's eye and pay no attention to the plank in your own eye?"
JESUS IN LUKE 6:41

Below, write down any ideas prompted by either these verses or the following questions...

_____

_____

_____

_____

_____

_____

What misunderstood Scripture verses can keep Christians in relationships with toxic people much longer than is necessary or healthy?

You can't change anyone; you can only change yourself. What is freeing—and what is convicting—about that truth?

If you are currently in a relationship with a toxic person, what is keeping you from pulling back or disconnecting? Are those reasons valid? Why or why not?

IN REAL LIFE

Two thousand years ago the apostle James wrote, "Be doers of the word, and not hearers only" (1:22). Reading and understanding the Bible is good, but it's not enough. We also need to put into action what we read. We need to be "doers of the word."

What idea from today's reading seems to be just for you?

What will you do in response to that insight? Be specific.

TALK IT THROUGH

We tend to make prayer more complicated than it needs to be. Prayer is simply having a conversation with God: we listen, and we speak.

LIFELINE
A person's toxicity is not about you.
Pull back. Disconnect. Let the toxic people go.

Listening
Spend a few minutes simply being quiet. As you consider the ideas in today's reading—including the LifeLine—what thoughts does God bring to mind? You may get a sense that you are to start doing something—or stop doing something. Perhaps you will recognize some changes that might be good to make.

Talking
Speak to God as if He is sitting right next to you—and use the everyday words you would use if you were talking to a friend. Thank God for what He has taught you about being in relationships with toxic people. Ask Him to help you use what you've learned. One of these may help you get started:

> Please give me compassion for the people I encounter as well as wisdom and courage to keep a healthy distance if necessary.

> When I slip into thinking that someone's toxicity is about me, please prompt me to pray for that person instead.

3
RELATIONSHIPS
DEALING WITH TOXIC PEOPLE

There's no other way to say it.... Passive-aggressive people are a whole new level of toxic. I know that from experience. Lots of experience.

Always trying to trick you or trip you up, passive-aggressive individuals disguise criticism with compliments. Or they have to have the last line in a conversation—and it's always an insult. Or they will be stubborn, wanting their way and not wanting me to have my way, thereby "proving" me wrong. Another type of passive-aggressive behavior is the indirect request that puts pressure on people to do a certain something: "It would be good to clean that bathroom today, but I guess next week will have to do." They want you to clean the bathroom—or deal with the guilt of letting them down.

Look at how Jesus handled the Pharisees who often tried to trick Him with their questions. They really didn't care about the answer. They wanted to get Jesus riled up or, later, trapped by His own words. But Jesus never let people manipulate Him with questions like that. He would not play their game. As Matthew reported, "Jesus knew their evil motives. 'You hypocrites!' He said. 'Whom are you trying to fool with your trick questions?'" (Matthew 22: 18 NLT).

Whenever the Pharisees tried to get Jesus in a corner, He always refused to debate them. Jesus' approach silenced them: you can't argue with someone who won't argue back. So when the Pharisees asked Jesus a question, He usually responded with a question that silenced them.

In Luke 6, for instance, we read about Jesus and His disciples walking through a grain field on the Sabbath. The Twelve were picking some heads of grain, rubbing them in their hands, and then eating the kernels. The Pharisees confronted Jesus: "Why are you doing what is unlawful on the Sabbath?" Jesus answered them, "Have you never read what David did when he and his companions were hungry? He entered the house of God, and taking the consecrated bread, he ate what is lawful only for priests to eat." (v. 2–4). The discussion was over.

Another day some chief priests and teachers of the law approached Jesus as he was teaching and preaching in the temple courts. "Tell us by what authority you are doing these things," they said. "Who gave you this authority?" [Jesus] replied, "I will also ask you a question. Tell me, John's baptism—was it from heaven, or from men?" (Luke 20:1–4). After acknowledging among themselves the crowd's response to either of the two answers, these Jewish leaders answered with "We don't know where it was from" (v. 7). If they didn't answer, neither would Jesus. Case closed.

Jesus did not engage with toxic people. He would not get hooked by their efforts to trap Him or anger Him. He would not engage with them.

And you don't have to either. Refuse to play the game of the toxic people in your life.

> **REFUSE TO PLAY THE GAME OF THE TOXIC PEOPLE IN YOUR LIFE.**

That strategy often involves setting boundaries. No one can pressure you without your permission. You can either listen to or not listen to their expectations. Don't let anybody enslave you to their expectations.

How many times in your life have you done something you didn't want to do, when you didn't have the time to do it, when there wasn't a good reason to do it, and/or when it wasn't really something you're gifted to do? But you did it because somebody had an expectation, and fulfilling that expectation was easier than saying no. I'll be blunt: you wasted that part of your life.

Learn to say no to unrealistic expectations. Set boundaries that limit your interactions with toxic, demanding people. Don't let such people enslave you with their expectations.

Although the apostle Paul was talking about freedom from the Old

Testament law, the principle works for toxic people: "Freedom is what we have—Christ has set us free! Stand, then, as free people, and do not allow yourselves to become slaves again" (Galatians 5:1 GNT).

Don't let any peer pressure put you into bondage. Christ set you free. You don't have to live according to the expectations of others.

LIFELINE
Refuse to play the game of toxic behaviors. Set boundaries to your interactions with them.

DIGGING DEEPER

LIFELINE
Refuse to play the game of toxic behaviors.
Set boundaries to your interactions with them.

Stay away from foolish people; they have nothing to teach you.
PROVERBS 14:7 GNT

As iron sharpens iron,
so one person sharpens another.
PROVERBS 27:17

Do not be misled: "Bad company corrupts good character."
1 CORINTHIANS 15:33

Below, write down any ideas prompted by either these verses or the following questions…

_____
_____
_____
_____
_____
_____
_____
_____

What, if anything, are you currently involved in because you weren't able to say no to someone's expectations? Why will—or why might—this experience help you say no next time?

Who in your life has been or is iron sharpening your iron, someone who challenges you to live more committed to Jesus and more reflective of His ways? Give an example or two.

What are some boundary-setting and boundary-maintaining statements that would be good to have ready when you need them?

IN REAL LIFE

Two thousand years ago the apostle James wrote, "Be doers of the word, and not hearers only" (1:22). Reading and understanding the Bible is good, but it's not enough. We also need to put into action what we read. We need to be "doers of the word."

What idea from today's reading seems to be just for you?

What will you do in response to that insight? Be specific.

TALK IT THROUGH

We tend to make prayer more complicated than it needs to be. Prayer is simply having a conversation with God: we listen, and we speak.

LIFELINE
Refuse to play the game of toxic behaviors. Set boundaries to your interactions with them.

Listening
Spend a few minutes simply being quiet. As you consider the ideas in today's reading—including the LifeLine—what thoughts does God bring to mind? You may get a sense that you are to start doing something—or stop doing something. Perhaps you will recognize some changes that might be good to make.

Talking
Speak to God as if He is sitting right next to you—and use the everyday words you would use if you were talking to a friend. Thank God for what He has taught you about how to deal wisely with toxic people. Ask Him to help you use what you've learned. One of these may help you get started:

Lord, You know what is fueling the toxic behavior and game playing of people in my life. I ask You to bless them with healing and freedom.

You promise to give wisdom when we ask, and I am asking You for wisdom so I can effectively establish boundaries and maintain them.

4
RELATIONSHIPS
WISDOM FOR RELATIONSHIPS

It takes me about seven minutes to drive home from my office. Years ago I started to use this time to clear my mind. I roll down the window and, figuratively speaking, toss out everything that has held onto me all day long. Most of the time it's the stress of someone's life problem that is, frankly, heartbreaking, or I'm thinking about an ongoing issue with a staff member. Throwing these matters out the window keeps me from dragging the day's problems into the most important relationships in my life. I have learned the wisdom of letting go before I reenter those relationships I value.

The apostle James offers us additional "wisdom that comes from heaven" that can also help us in our relationships. He begins by saying that this heavenly wisdom is "first of all pure" (James 3:17).

Pure means "uncorrupted, authentic." In 1 John 3:3 this word refers to Jesus' character, and at the heart of the issue for His followers is what I consider a twenty-first-century equivalent: integrity. If I am wise about relationships, I will be authentic, genuine, transparent, and honest, as Jesus was. I'm not going to lie to you, I'm not going to cheat you, I'm not going to manipulate you, I'm not going to be deceitful: I will be a person of integrity, as Jesus was. After all, every healthy relationship is built on trust and respect. If you aren't honest, who is going to trust you? If you aren't honest, who is going to respect you? To have healthy relationships—to succeed in life—we have to live with integrity.

We live out our relationships the way David and Jonathan did: with integrity, honesty, and trust. Jonathan—King Saul's son and the bloodline successor to the throne—and David—the man God had chosen and anointed to be king—form an unlikely friendship with Jonathan eventually helping David escape from his murderous father. Consider their farewell:

> **TO HAVE HEALTHY RELATIONSHIPS—TO SUCCEED IN LIFE— WE HAVE TO LIVE WITH INTEGRITY.**

> *They kissed each other and wept together—but David wept the most.*
>
> *Jonathan said to David, "Go in peace, for we have sworn friendship with each other in the name of the LORD, saying, 'The LORD is a witness between you and me, and between your descendants and my descendants forever.'"*
> **1 SAMUEL 20:41-42**

In addition to living with the integrity that facilitates soul connections as David and Jonathan experienced, it is also wise to work to maintain harmony in our relationships. I won't always be looking for a fight, and I won't make you angry because—as James wrote—"wisdom is ... peace-loving" (James 3:17).

Have you ever met someone who is always arguing, always looking for a fight? I heard about one guy who was so argumentative he would only eat food that disagreed with him. Seriously, if you're smart, you don't antagonize people—and you don't let other people spark your anger. Solomon—the author of the wisdom book of Proverbs—commented on both:

> *Any fool can start arguments; the honorable [wise] thing is to stay out of them.*
> **PROVERBS 20:3 GNT**

> *A wise man controls his temper. He knows that anger causes mistakes.*
> **PROVERBS 14:29 TLB**

Anger causes mistakes in relationships, so a wise believer works to maintain harmony.

In addition to being pure and peace-loving, relational wisdom is considerate and courteous. And those traits are not evident when people play the game My Day Was Worse Than Your Day, yet spouses are often really good at it.

You know, the husband comes home from work, exhausted, and the game begins: "The traffic was awful, a major client backed out of a deal, and of course my boss got upset." The wife hits the ball back: "Oh, yeah? Junior dunked the cat down the toilet, the beans burned, and the babysitter canceled."

The fact is, both the husband and the wife had a tough day. When that happens, wisdom is considerate: allow your spouse to be tired without having to say, "I'm more tired that you are." The fact is, you're both tired. Simply—and compassionately—acknowledge the other person's exhaustion or frustration rather than turning the conversation into a competition.

If I am wise, I will be mindful of and value the other person's feelings. If I'm wise, I won't minimize your feelings or dismiss them as being invalid, illogical, irrational, or silly. I don't have to understand why you feel the way you do, but I can respect that you do have those feelings. So I will be considerate.

LIFELINE
Be wise in relationships by being a person of integrity, working to maintain harmony, and respecting the other person's feelings.

DIGGING DEEPER

LIFELINE
Be wise in relationships by being a person of integrity, working to maintain harmony, and respecting the other person's feelings.

Whoever walks in integrity walks securely.
PROVERBS 10:9

"In everything, do to others what you would have them do to you."
JESUS IN MATTHEW 7:12

Show proper respect to everyone, love the family of believers, fear God, honor the emperor.
1 PETER 2:17

Below, write down any ideas prompted by either these verses or the following questions...

Comment on the value our culture places on integrity and on its prevalence or absence.

Why can it be difficult to respect another person's emotions? What can we do to overcome those difficulties?

IN REAL LIFE

Two thousand years ago the apostle James wrote, "Be doers of the word, and not hearers only" (1:22). Reading and understanding the Bible is good, but it's not enough. We also need to put into action what we read. We need to be "doers of the word."

What idea from today's reading seems to be just for you?

What will you do in response to that insight? Be specific.

TALK IT THROUGH

We tend to make prayer more complicated than it needs to be. Prayer is simply having a conversation with God: we listen, and we speak.

LIFELINE
Be wise in relationships by being a person of integrity, working to maintain harmony, and respecting the other person's feelings.

Listening
Spend a few minutes simply being quiet. As you consider the ideas in today's reading—including the LifeLine—what thoughts does God bring to mind? You may get a sense that you are to start doing something—or stop doing something. Perhaps you will recognize some changes that might be good to make.

Talking
Speak to God as if He is sitting right next to you—and use the everyday words you would use if you were talking to a friend. Thank God for what He has taught you about relationships. Ask Him to help you use what you've learned. One of these may help you get started:

Please keep me strong when I'm tempted to compromise my integrity; to choose selfishness over harmony in the relationship, and to belittle or dismiss the other person's feelings.

Enable me—teach me—to love others with Your love and to treat them the way I would want them to treat me.

5
RELATIONSHIPS
LIFE-CHANGING ACCEPTANCE

I regularly remind the people in my church, "Don't judge people who sin differently than you do."

That one statement says a lot about how to relate to people, doesn't it? If we take this one thought with us into all of our relationships, we would be slow to judge, quick to forgive, and free to love. And I believe that these actions reflect what wisdom in relationships looks like.

We also reveal our wisdom about relationships when we are reasonable, when we aren't defensive or stubborn, when we are open to logic, ideas, and suggestions, and when we are willing to listen and learn from others. The Revised Standard Version says that wisdom is "open to reason"; the Living Bible says that wisdom "allows discussion."

Consider the new pastor's wise response on his first Sunday. A man walked out of church, shook the pastor's hand, and said, "Pastor, that sermon stunk."

Trying to be open, reasonable, and wise, the pastor asked, "What didn't you like about it?"

"First, you read it. Second, you read it poorly. And, third, it wasn't worth reading in the first place."

Another man walked out right behind him and said, "Don't listen to old Jim. He just repeats what he hears everybody else say."

If you're wise, you'll be open to suggestions. As Solomon observed, "A fool thinks he needs no advice, but a wise man listens to others" (Proverbs 12:15 TLB). A wise person won't get defensive or respond with criticism, but he or she will exercise discernment to see how valid the comment was, if at all. To be specific, if what a person says is true, listen and learn from it. If it's false, ignore it and forget it and move on. That is wisdom in relationships.

Choose to forgive the other person's mistakes. James put it this way: "Wisdom is… full of mercy and good fruit" (James 3:17). Forgiveness is definitely good fruit!

Does that describe you—or do you jump on people every time they stumble, every time they make a mistake, show a flaw, or misspeak? Wisdom is full of mercy: it doesn't dwell on or emphasize a person's mistakes. Are you merciful in your relationships, or do you hound people about their past mistakes? Again, note Solomon's wisdom: "Love forgets mistakes; nagging about them parts the best of friends" (Proverbs 17:9 TLB).

When somebody stumbles, let's not judge them. Let's encourage them instead. None of us needs judgment when we stumble; that's when we especially need encouragement. And that encouragement is one of the good fruits of wisdom. We are kind with our words and our actions, offering support, prayer, our time, and our companionship.

> **WHEN SOMEBODY STUMBLES, LET'S NOT JUDGE THEM. LET'S ENCOURAGE THEM INSTEAD.**

Finally, more evidence of wisdom in relationships is honesty about our weaknesses. Wise people don't try to hide or disguise their weaknesses. They choose not to hide behind the masks of hypocrisy or insincerity. They don't try to hide behind different masks depending on the people they are with.

Sometimes—as Jesus' life models for us—it takes the wholehearted acceptance of someone who sees our weaknesses to enable us to be open about them. Consider some of the people whom Jesus, Friend of sinners, spent time with: Matthew was a tax collector, Saul was a murderer of Jesus-followers, several middle-class fishermen became His disciples, Jesus showed compassion for prostitutes, He reached out to a Samaritan woman at the well, He healed the Roman centurion's servant, and, very counter-culturally, He chose to appear first to a woman—Mary Magdalene— after He rose from the dead.

Jesus was well aware of both the weaknesses and the sins of the people He interacted with. And as the gospel accounts of His life clearly indicate, again and again, Jesus' love and acceptance were life-changing blessings to those individuals blessed by His love. Similarly, our being accepted by Jesus and by others can change our lives, and our Christlike acceptance of people despite their weaknesses and sins can be life-changing for them.

Being honest and genuine with people about our weaknesses and strengths will free and even encourage them to be more honest and genuine about their own weaknesses and strengths. That kind of openness and honesty are foundational for relationships in which the individuals involved can be iron sharpening iron just as God intends.

LIFELINE
Be wise in relationships by being nonjudgmental and reasonable, forgiving the other person's mistakes, and being honest about your weaknesses.

DIGGING DEEPER

LIFELINE
Be wise in relationships by being nonjudgmental and reasonable, forgiving the other person's mistakes, and being honest about your weaknesses.

"Do not judge, or you too will be judged. For in the same way you judge others, you will be judged, and with the measure you use, it will be measured to you."
JESUS IN MATTHEW 7:1-2

Peter came to Jesus and asked, "Lord, how many times shall I forgive my brother or sister who sins against me? Up to seven times?"

Jesus answered, "I tell you, not seven times, but seventy-seven times."
MATTHEW 18:21-22

Everyone should be quick to listen, slow to speak and slow to become angry.
JAMES 1:19

Below, write down any ideas prompted by either these verses or the following questions...

Why is it so easy to judge others? Why is it so difficult for us to evaluate how reasonable we are or aren't being?

Why is forgiveness important for the person being forgiven as well as for the person doing the forgiving?

Why can honesty about our weaknesses build bridges between us and other people?

IN REAL LIFE

Two thousand years ago the apostle James wrote, "Be doers of the word, and not hearers only" (1:22). Reading and understanding the Bible is good, but it's not enough. We also need to put into action what we read. We need to be "doers of the word."

What idea from today's reading seems to be just for you?

What will you do in response to that insight? Be specific.

TALK IT THROUGH

We tend to make prayer more complicated than it needs to be. Prayer is simply having a conversation with God: we listen, and we speak.

LIFELINE
Be wise in relationships by being nonjudgmental and reasonable, forgiving the other person's mistakes, and being honest about your weaknesses.

Listening
Spend a few minutes simply being quiet. As you consider the ideas in today's reading—including the LifeLine—what thoughts does God bring to mind? You may get a sense that you are to start doing something—or stop doing something. Perhaps you will recognize some changes that might be good to make.

Talking
Speak to God as if He is sitting right next to you—and use the everyday words you would use if you were talking to a friend. Thank God for what He has taught you about relationships. Ask Him to help you use what you've learned. One of these may help you get started:

I find it so easy to see other people's sins. Please help me see mine, repent, and live differently.

Being Christ-like in my relationships means being humble. Please help me remember how small I am by living with a keen awareness of how great and glorious You are.

THE WEEK IN REVIEW

LIFELINES for Relationships

Beware of people who are legalistic, hypocritical, faultfinding, and guilt-tripping—and of becoming one yourself.

▶

A person's toxicity is not about you. Pull back. Disconnect. Let the toxic people go.

▶

Refuse to play the game of toxic behaviors. Set boundaries to your interactions with them.

▶

Be wise in relationships by being a person of integrity, working to maintain harmony, and respecting the other person's feelings.

▶

Be wise in relationships by being nonjudgmental and reasonable, forgiving the other person's mistakes, and being honest about your weaknesses.

For Personal Reflection or Group Discussion

The Holy Spirit can reveal our sin to us, but what is the value of having a flesh-and-blood person in your life who can help you see where you are being legalistic, judgmental, hypocritical?

What are three or four reasons why it's important to understand that you can't control anyone else's behavior or change anyone else?

What is your experience with passive-aggressive people? What is a Christ-like way to respond to them?

What are some healthy boundaries to set with toxic people—and what are some ways to communicate those boundaries to those people?

When listening to others what can you do to make other's feel heard and respected?

Unpack the statement "Don't judge people who sin differently than you do." Why can be accepted by someone who knows quite well your weaknesses and even your sins be utterly life-changing? (To whom can you give that gift?)

1
TIME
HOW ARE YOU?

It's an iconic circus image. The lion tamer—of course wearing a red jacket—holds a stool and a whip as he walks toward the lion's cage. Have you ever wondered why he takes a stool with him when he steps into the cage? Because a stool has proven to tame a lion better than anything.

Why is a stool so effective? Because when the trainer holds the stool with its legs pointing toward the lion's face, the animal tries to focus on all four legs of the stool at once—and the king of beasts just can't do it! The stool's four legs confuse the lion; it is paralyzed by uncertainty. So the lion tamer is safe: the distracted lion will not attack.

> **WE HUMAN BEINGS CAN FIND OUR DIVIDED FOCUS PARALYZING US.**

I share this story because, in the same way, we human beings can find our divided focus paralyzing us.

Maybe you can't identify with the lion. Then let me share another iconic image that we… uh… vintage people will remember. I'm talking about *The Ed Sullivan Show*, a variety show that ran from June 1948 (only black-and-white TV!) to June 1971 (living color!). Ed Sullivan hosted a wide range of acts—and his was, in fact, the program that introduced the Beatles to the US. But I digress…

One of Ed Sullivan's most memorable acts was a man who would spin plates. I'll explain: This man had a long row of wooden dowels standing vertically on the stage. Starting at one end, he'd set a plate on top of the dowel and get it spinning. Then he would move on the next dowel and get another plate spinning. Of course, as soon as he had a half-dozen or so spinning, the plates he had first gotten spinning would start to wobble, and he'd run back to the end to get them spinning again. Soon he was running back and forth like crazy to keep all of his plates from crashing into a million pieces on the stage floor. (Yes, you can google this *Ed Sullivan Show* act and see the tuxedoed and talented plate-spinner perform.)

I dusted off that story from the archives because it's a perfect picture of what life is too often like… for too many of us. Not convinced? Think about the response

> **THINK ABOUT THE RESPONSE YOU MAY GET WHEN YOU SIMPLY ASK, "HOW ARE YOU?" "FINE" USED TO BE THE AUTOMATIC ANSWER, BUT VERY OFTEN IN THIS ERA, THE ANSWER IS "BUSY" INSTEAD.**

you may get when you simply ask, "How are you?" "Fine" used to be the automatic answer, but very often in this era, the answer is "Busy" instead. All of us are probably spinning at least a few too many plates. And we're exhausted. And, like the lion, probably not very focused and perhaps even paralyzed.

If you can relate to the plate spinner or the lion, that divided focus and the exhaustion from running around are signs that you could probably do a better job of guarding your time. I want to encourage you—and I'm talking to myself as well—to limit the number of plates you're trying to keep spinning at any one particular time. Learn to say no to the good, the worthwhile, and the useful so that you are free to say yes to the best. And that is today's LifeLine—and it is definitely worth repeating (and perhaps even tattooing on your arm): Say yes to the best.

And now I'll get practical. One idea today; more tomorrow.

Today's suggestion: Focus on your passion. Often that corresponds with what you are gifted in or a skill you have developed. All of us can do things that we don't enjoy, and sometimes we have to. It's part of life. But over time, if we are spending many hours and lots of energy keeping plates spinning in areas that don't energize and refresh us, we are setting ourselves up for burnout… and worse.

So consider today's thoughts my very countercultural permission to just have a few plates spinning at any one time. Fewer plates will mean a sharper focus... greater effectiveness in your efforts... and greater satisfaction with life.

And who doesn't want that?

LIFELINE
Learn to say no to the good, the worthwhile, and the useful so that you are free to say yes to the best.

DIGGING DEEPER

LIFELINE
Learn to say no to the good, the worthwhile, and the useful so that you are free to say yes to the best.

Teach us to number our days, that we may gain a heart of wisdom.
PSALM 90:12

The LORD gives wisdom; from his mouth come knowledge and understanding.
PROVERBS 2:6

If any of you lacks wisdom, you should ask God, who gives generously to all without finding fault, and it will be given to you.
JAMES 1:5

Below, write down any ideas prompted by either these verses or the following questions...

Why do you struggle—if you do struggle—to say no? If you are able to say no, what good in your life has resulted from that skill?

What can you do to discern the good from the best?

Think of a wise person you know. What did he/she do to become wise? If you don't know, ask.

IN REAL LIFE

Two thousand years ago the apostle James wrote, "Be doers of the word, and not hearers only" (1:22). Reading and understanding the Bible is good, but it's not enough. We also need to put into action what we read. We need to be "doers of the word."

What idea from today's reading seems to be just for you?

What step will you take in response to that insight? Be specific.

TALK IT THROUGH

We tend to make prayer more complicated than it needs to be. Prayer is simply having a conversation with God: we listen, and we speak.

LIFELINE
Learn to say no to the good, the worthwhile, and the useful so that you are free to say yes to the best.

Listening
Spend a few minutes simply being quiet. As you consider the ideas in today's reading—including the LifeLine—what thoughts does God bring to mind? You may get a sense that you are to start doing something—or stop doing something. Perhaps you will recognize some changes that might be good to make.

Talking
Speak to God as if He is sitting right next to you—and use the everyday words you would use if you were talking to a friend. Thank God for what He has taught you about your use of time. Ask Him to help you use what you've learned. One of these may help you get started:

Please help me recognize—and help me let go of—the wrong reasons I struggle to say no.

Teach me to develop the ability to differentiate between the good and the best.

2

TIME

SAYING NO TO THE GOOD AND YES TO THE BEST

So did you identify more with the plate spinner or the lion? The plate spinner was doing too much, and the lion—not knowing what to focus on—was paralyzed. Are you more a crazed plate spinner or an immobilized lion? Neither is good....

To avoid both, we do well to focus our time on what we're passionate about, on activities that undoubtedly energize and refresh us. And focusing on our passions will be easier if we have fewer plates spinning at any one time. So—and this is the first of today's practical points—we need to say no to some of the plates we're invited to spin and instead use that time to rest.

The precedent has definitely been set. If you look at Jesus' life, you'll see that He often took time to rest. No one in history accomplished more than Jesus did—and He did so without getting an ulcer. Also, where did we get the idea that relaxation is selfish? The truth is, there's nothing productive about a heart attack, and there's nothing good about a nervous breakdown. Give yourself permission to say no and to relax.

Rest allows us to recharge our batteries and reevaluate how well we're living out our priorities. Our Creator God knows how important rest is. In fact, one of His Ten Commandments—right up there with commands like "Don't murder"—is to keep a Sabbath, to set aside a day to rest and to connect with God, your family, and yourself. The American version of a weekend bears little resemblance to a Sabbath rest. Oil changes, youth sports, household chores, yard work—these are just some of the activities that can overfill our weekends.

This week, try something different. Block out some time—maybe Saturday morning or Sunday afternoon—to do absolutely nothing. No TV. No activities. Not even a book to read. Just sit and relax. Listen for God as you consider your life. When you make time to rest, you're probably saying no to some good things, but you're saying yes to the better.

Another way to say no to the lesser and yes to the better is to make a list every day of the things you need to get done that day. If you're a salesperson, your list might include five new client sales calls, plus a half-dozen follow-up calls and three notes to current clients. If you're a business owner, you may list two hours of reading about new markets, an hour spent with your CFO to look at increased efficiencies, and three calls about a potential merger or acquisition. Whatever the specifics, get down on paper those tasks you need to take care of before the end of the workday—and then do the most difficult item first. Do absolutely nothing else until you've crossed that one off. When you do the hardest thing first, you'll be amazed by how the rest of your day falls into place. Not having that task hanging over you helps you focus on other things you need to get done.

> **WHEN YOU DO THE HARDEST THING FIRST, YOU'LL BE AMAZED BY HOW THE REST OF YOUR DAY FALLS INTO PLACE.**

Finally, as we consider how we are using our time, we do well to open the book of Ecclesiastes. In addition to saying a lot about meaningless pursuits and the fleeting nature of life, the book calls us—as the entire Bible does—to invest our lives in what matters, in what will last for eternity.

As I understand it, only two things will last forever: the Word of God, and the souls of people. Nothing else—not money, houses, or businesses—will last. Even your body will wear out, and you'll be carried to your final resting place by six relatives or friends.

Knowing what will last and what won't, I'm able to spend my life investing in the eternal future—and you are too. The time I spend meditating on God's Word and sharing His love will pay dividends in this life as well as for eternity.

When we let ourselves say no to the good, the worthwhile, the useful, we are freer to say yes to the best. When we have a better command of our time, we will also do a better job with our health, our relationships, our work, and even our money. (LifeLines for those topics to come!)

Right now let's focus on not getting sidetracked by things that don't matter. You have one life. Invest it well.

LIFELINE
Don't let yourself get sidetracked by things that don't matter. You have one life. Invest it well.

DIGGING DEEPER

LIFELINE
Don't let yourself get sidetracked by things that don't matter. You have one life. Invest it well.

Choose this day whom you will serve.
JOSHUA 24:15 ESV

The grass withers, the flower fades, but the word of our God will stand forever.
ISAIAH 40:8 ESV

"You have six days in which to do your work, but the seventh day is a day of rest dedicated to Me."
EXODUS 20:9-10 GNT

Below, write down any ideas prompted by either these verses or the following questions...

_____
_____
_____
_____
_____
_____
_____

Look at your calendar and your QuickBooks or checkbook register. Whom or what are you serving? In other words, what priorities are reflected there?

Who has invested his/her life in you? What did that investing look like? What were the results?

What words about your life would you like to have written on your tombstone?

IN REAL LIFE

Two thousand years ago the apostle James wrote, "Be doers of the word, and not hearers only" (1:22). Reading and understanding the Bible is good, but it's not enough. We also need to put into action what we read. We need to be "doers of the word."

What idea from today's reading seems to be just for you?

What will you do in response to that insight? Be specific.

TALK IT THROUGH

LIFELINE
Don't let yourself get sidetracked by things that don't matter. You have one life. Invest it well.

We tend to make prayer more complicated than it needs to be. Prayer is simply having a conversation with God: we listen, and we speak.

Listening
Spend a few minutes simply being quiet. As you consider the ideas in today's reading—including the LifeLine—what thoughts does God bring to mind? You may get a sense that you are to start doing something—or stop doing something. Perhaps you will recognize some changes that might be good to make.

Talking
Speak to God as if He is sitting right next to you—and use the everyday words you would use if you were talking to a friend. Thank God for what He has taught you about your use of time. Ask Him to help you use what you've learned. One of these may help you get started:

Lord, teach me to invest my time wisely in Your Word and in people.

Please give me the faith I need to stop working and rest—faith that You will enable everything that needs to be done to get done. Please give me the faith I need to be able to rest.

3

TIME

A LIFE OUT OF BALANCE

We eat fast food. We use Quicken to computerize our finances. We use speed-dial to call people. And some brave souls swim wearing a... Speedo.

All too easily, the fast pace of our world causes our lives to get out of balance. Consider the warning our cars offer. When we get new tires, they need to get balanced. If we skip this step, we're going to have a bumpy ride, and—more seriously—that out-of-balance tire will eventually wear out, if not blow out.

While out-of-balance tires blow out, out-of-balance people burn out. How close to burnout are you? Are you moving too fast? The following four touchpoints can be your speedometer.

First, when we move too fast, *we get stressed out.*

We all know stress—work deadlines to meet, the boss's demands to satisfy, relationships to invest in, kids to raise, a home and cars to maintain, financial stress, and the list goes on. As the pace intensifies and the stress grows and you may find yourself thinking, "I wasn't made to live this way."

And you weren't. This pace costs us many things, one of which is mentioned in Song of Solomon 1:6—"I had no time to care for myself" (GNT).

When you don't have any time to care for yourself—when you don't have time to work out, go for a walk, meet a friend for coffee, or read the paper—the stress mounts. And we know that all too often it's a little thing that puts you over the edge.

Second, when we move too fast, *we lose joy.*

The faster we move through life, the less time we have to notice the blessings and to enjoy the life God has given us. Think about it. When was the last time you felt genuine joy?

Although his life was short on joy and blessings for quite a season, Job knew what we're talking about. He said, "My days go by faster than a runner; they fly away without my seeing any joy" (Job 9:25 NCV).

If your days are flying by and you're not seeing joy, know—as I said earlier—that God didn't create you to live this way. Let me offer as evidence that He wants you to slow down: the bones in fish, the seeds in watermelon, and that little pain you get in your head when you eat ice cream too fast. Slow down so you can know joy.

When we move too fast, *we are less productive.*

> **SLOW DOWN SO YOU CAN KNOW JOY.**

That sounds counterintuitive, but it's true. We live as if the faster we go, the more we'll get done, but actually, the faster we go, the less productive we become. If we run too fast, we experience the law of diminishing returns. We can't think anymore. We can't create any more.

As Solomon observed in Proverbs 21:5, "Careful planning puts you ahead in the long run; hurry and scurry puts you further behind" (MSG).

And, in Alice in Wonderland, the White Rabbit said it this way: "The hurrier I go, the behinder I get." Because of the fast pace of our lives, many of us feel just as the White Rabbit did.

We need to hear—and live by—the truth that God didn't make us to keep on going and going and going. He created us human beings with a built-in need to rest and recharge. That recharging may be as unique as our fingerprints, but the need to recharge is an unchanging part of being human. Know when to say, "I need to rest."

When we move too fast, *we can't hear God.*

It makes absolute sense that when we're moving too fast, juggling too many balls, trying to focus on too many things, we don't hear the voice of God. Sometimes God is trying to get a message through to us, but all the circuits are busy and we can't hear it. That's why we are wise to frequently, regularly obey His command "Be still, and know that I am God" (Psalm 46:10 NIV).

When was the last time you took time to be still?

A life out of balance leads to stress, joylessness, less productivity, and the inability to hear God's voice. Consider, then, what a life in balance would hold! Less stress, more joy, greater productivity, and the ability to hear God's guiding voice of love. Why not give it a try?

LIFELINE
We are wise to frequently and regularly obey His command "Be still, and know that I am God" (Psalm 46:10).

DIGGING DEEPER

LIFELINE
We are wise to frequently and regularly obey His command "Be still, and know that I am God" (Psalm 46:10).

*Come, let us bow down in worship,
let us kneel before the LORD, our Maker!*
PSALM 95:6

You make [me] glad with the joy of your presence.
PSALM 21:6 ESV

*The LORD is my strength and my shield;
my heart trusts in him, and he helps me.*

*My heart leaps for joy,
and with my song I praise him.*
PSALM 28:7

Below, write down any ideas prompted by either these verses or the following questions...

_____

_____

_____

_____

_____

_____

What drives and/or significantly contributes to your busyness? A schedule that has simply become too full? The culture's message? If you're active in a church, the church itself? Something else?

What—if anything—internal seems to drive and/or significantly contribute to your busyness? Your personality? Your woundedness? Your fear? Something else?

Why is it important—even essential—for you to be still and spend time with God?

IN REAL LIFE

Two thousand years ago the apostle James wrote, "Be doers of the word, and not hearers only" (1:22). Reading and understanding the Bible is good, but it's not enough. We also need to put into action what we read. We need to be "doers of the word."

What idea from today's reading seems to be just for you?

What will you do in response to that insight? Be specific.

TALK IT THROUGH

We tend to make prayer more complicated than it needs to be. Prayer is simply having a conversation with God: we listen, and we speak.

LIFELINE
We are wise to frequently and regularly obey His command "Be still, and know that I am God" (Psalm 46:10).

Listening
Spend a few minutes simply being quiet. As you consider the ideas in today's reading—including the LifeLine—what thoughts does God bring to mind? You may get a sense that you are to start doing something—or stop doing something. Perhaps you will recognize some changes that might be good to make.

Talking
Speak to God as if He is sitting right next to you—and use the everyday words you would use if you were talking to a friend. Thank God for what He has taught you about your use of time. Ask Him to help you use what you've learned. One of these may help you get started:

Please help me to understand why I keep the pace I do and to recognize what changes You would have me make.

I ask You to show me when and where I can regularly "be still" and spend time with You.

4

TIME

FINDING BALANCE

I have a one-word suggestion for how we can use our time wisely and well. That word is order.

Order is doing the right thing... at the right time... in the right way.

Order in traffic protects drivers and pedestrians. Order in business prevents financial mistakes. Order in relationships diminishes conflict. Order in your environment creates comfort.

Order is also a key to your productivity in life. Living an orderly life will enable you to be more effective with the days and years God has given you. And He will help you bring order to your life. After all, "God is not a God of disorder but of peace" (1 Corinthians 14:33).

When you start putting your life in order, you are deciding what you want to experience every day. Putting your life in order also allows you to establish healthy habits: you find time to work out, read a book, and hang out with friends.

Being able to say no helps us establish that kind of order in our lives. But saying no may be difficult if we're addicted to a fast-paced life and the adrenaline that results. If saying no in the moment and directly to the person making the request is difficult, buy yourself some time by saying that you'll think it over—and be sure to follow up. You might also say that you don't think you can add another item to your schedule or another commitment to your calendar. If the request is something you want to pursue, mention that another time would work better for you. Say, "Not yet" instead of no.

Above all, do what you can to avoid saying yes if doing so would be unhealthy. As Proverbs 20:25 says, "An impulsive vow is a trap; later you'll wish you could get out of it" (MSG). I'm guessing you've had occasions to think, Why did I say yes to that? Why am I doing this? Don't promise without pondering. Don't decide without deliberating. Make commitments carefully.

And don't overdo those commitments because—as I've mentioned before—you need time to rest and to sleep. Both bring healing to your body and new energy for all that life holds. Furthermore, when we're tired, we think differently—as in, not very rationally or clearly. We talk differently—as in, not choosing our words very carefully. And we look at life differently—as in, without much optimism or hope. As Green Bay Packers coach Vince Lombardi (1913–1970) said, "Fatigue makes cowards of us all." Tiredness saps not only our courage but also our faith. When fatigue walks in, faith walks out.

Clearly, we need to rest and sleep. Both enable us to rest our bodies, recharge our emotions and refocus our spirits. Both help us have the patience we need when we find ourselves waiting on God.

Very few people enjoy those seasons of waiting that build our trust in God, but know that He has good plans for you and a perfect timetable for fulfilling those plans. He never tells us that timetable because He wants us to trust Him.

Second, don't forget that God has your best interest at heart. And your best doesn't always mean fast, soon, or immediately. Ask yourself, "Is faster always better?" The answer is "Absolutely not." So trust God's timing.

OK, but what does waiting on God's perfect timing have to do with LifeLines for time? Good question. If you're serious about slowing the pace of your life, you need to take a deep breath and choose to trust that God has a plan for your life. You'll find it easier to trust your faithful God as you get to know Him better. Knowing the Bible better will reinforce the truth that God's timing is always perfect.

Recognize that God establishes the timing of all history and the timing of your life events. Living in light of that truth may help you slow your pace. After all, you can't speed up God's plans by racing toward your goals and dreams. So learn to wait on God's timing.

> **YOU CAN'T SPEED UP GOD'S PLANS BY RACING TOWARD YOUR GOALS AND DREAMS. SO LEARN TO WAIT ON GOD'S TIMING.**

Also, bring personal balance to your life. Get everything—your schedule, your relationships, your home, your work, your finances—in order. Make time for rest and sleep. And slow down your pace as you yield to God's perfect timing.

An out-of-balance life can squeeze the love, life, and laughter right out of you. But a balanced life frees you to laugh, to love, and to truly live.

LIFELINE
Don't promise without pondering.
Don't decide without deliberating.
Make commitments carefully.

DIGGING DEEPER

LIFELINE
Don't promise without pondering.
Don't decide without deliberating.
Make commitments carefully.

[God] does everything just right and on time, but people can never completely understand what he is doing.
ECCLESIASTES 3:11 NCV

God is not a God of disorder but of peace.
1 CORINTHIANS 14:33

Wait on the LORD: be of good courage, and he shall strengthen your heart: wait, I say, on the LORD!
PSALM 27:14 NKJV

Below, write down any ideas prompted by either these verses or the following questions...

What are some consequences you have experienced when you promised without pondering, decided without deliberating, or made commitments carelessly?

When have you seen God do something that in hindsight was His perfect timing even though that time frame was not what you had originally wanted?

What are you waiting for right now? Describe what you would like this season of waiting to be like.

IN REAL LIFE

Two thousand years ago the apostle James wrote, "Be doers of the word, and not hearers only" (1:22). Reading and understanding the Bible is good, but it's not enough. We also need to put into action what we read. We need to be "doers of the word."

What idea from today's reading seems to be just for you?

What will you do in response to that insight? Be specific.

TALK IT THROUGH

We tend to make prayer more complicated than it needs to be. Prayer is simply having a conversation with God: we listen, and we speak.

LIFELINE
Don't promise without pondering.
Don't decide without deliberating.
Make commitments carefully.

Listening
Spend a few minutes simply being quiet. As you consider the ideas in today's reading—including the LifeLine—what thoughts does God bring to mind? You may get a sense that you are to start doing something—or stop doing something. Perhaps you will recognize some changes that might be good to make.

Talking
Speak to God as if He is sitting right next to you—and use the everyday words you would use if you were talking to a friend. Thank God for what He has taught you about your use of time. Ask Him to help you use what you've learned. One of these may help you get started:

Lord, You know the decision(s) I face right now. Please help me be sensitive to Your guidance as I consider my options.

As I think about when I wasn't careful about a decision, show me the lesson(s) You want me to take away from that experience.

5

TIME

WHY ARE WE PUSHING SO HARD?

If you're serious about bringing a healthy balance to your life, you're going to have to look honestly at your motivations and your values. What's driving you? What motivates you? Everything is secondary until you consider your motives, your values, and—more often than not today—your constant push for more.

Why do we find ourselves constantly pushing for more? It seems as if we are always working toward having more advancement in our career, more money in our bank accounts, more activities and gatherings in our schedules, and more ways to post it all on Instagram. Do you find yourself constantly asking for more in your own life? Only you can answer that question.

One reason for this push—the reason we'll focus on today—is ambition. Webster's defines ambition as "an ardent desire for rank, fame, or power; desire to achieve a particular end." There's nothing wrong with ambition—in moderation. In and of itself, ambition is a good thing: it's why things get done in the world. Furthermore, our good God created each one of us to be ambitious in certain areas.

But ambition that is out of control, ambition without boundaries, ambition fueled by immoral motivations or values is probably one of the most destructive forces in the universe. Out-of-control ambition destroys lives, it destroys families, and it destroys marriages. It can destroy countries when an overly ambitious leader becomes a dictator.

Also, not all high achievers should be admired. They may be pushing themselves for unhealthy reasons or wrong motives. Ambition can be driven by guilt, by resentment, by fear, by revenge, and by ego. Ambition can be driven by pride, by "I'll show them! I'll show my parents! I'm going to show that teacher who said I'd never amount to anything. I'm going to show my brother and sister." Ambition can be driven by anger. Clearly, not all ambition is good.

> **NOT ALL HIGH ACHIEVERS SHOULD BE ADMIRED.**

The starting point for slowing down the pace of your life is to not clear your schedule. You can go home today and clear the calendar for the next three months—and it would fill up very quickly again because you haven't dealt with the root issue of why you are so driven. Why do you take on more than you really need to take on? Why do you pursue more business, more clients, more whatever even when it's harming you emotionally and spiritually? Even when it's damaging your relationships or destroying your health?

The starting point for getting balance in your life (I told you we'd get here) is not to clear the decks. The starting point is to choose to be content with who you are and with what you have. Until you reach that point, you will always be driven to take on more, and that constant push just isn't healthy. The writer of Ecclesiastes shared his perspective on this matter: "It is better to have only a little, with peace of mind, than be busy all the time" (4:6 GNT).

So ask yourself these tough questions: Will having more make me happier? Will doing more make me happier? Will having more activities make me happier?

The answer is no. More—of anything—will not make you happier. If you aren't happy with what you have today, you're not going to be happy with what you get tomorrow because today you're not happy with what you wanted yesterday and got. (It's OK to read that sentence again.) If you aren't happy with your circumstances now, you never will be because you are never going to have perfect circumstances.

Another way to end your constant pushing is to stop comparing yourself to other people. Those comparisons—"Look at what she has! Look at what they're doing!"—are the mortal enemy of contentment. Simply put, comparing ruins contentment. In fact, contentment comes more easily when you don't compare. (Maybe Facebook just isn't a healthy pastime.)

Proverbs 14:30 says, "A relaxed attitude lengthens a man's life; jealousy rots it away" (NLT). You can't be relaxed and jealous, relaxed and envious, or relaxed and in comparison mode at the same time.

God can help you rein in your ambition, help you choose contentment, and help you slow down.

LIFELINE

To start getting balance in your life, start choosing to be content with who you are and with what you have.

DIGGING DEEPER

LIFELINE
To start getting balance in your life, start choosing to be content with who you are and with what you have.

It is better to have only a little, with peace of mind, than be busy all the time.
ECCLESIASTES 4:6 (GNT)

*I praise you because I am fearfully and wonderfully made;
your works are wonderful;
I know that full well.*
PSALM 139:14

Godliness with contentment is a great gain.
1 TIMOTHY 6:6

Below, write down any ideas prompted by either these verses or the following questions...

Why can busyness prevent us from knowing contentment and peace?

What key to contentment does Psalm 139:14 offer?

Why can contentment be elusive?

IN REAL LIFE

Two thousand years ago the apostle James wrote, "Be doers of the word, and not hearers only" (1:22). Reading and understanding the Bible is good, but it's not enough. We also need to put into action what we read. We need to be "doers of the word."

What idea from today's reading seems to be just for you?

What will you do in response to that insight? Be specific.

TALK IT THROUGH

We tend to make prayer more complicated than it needs to be. Prayer is simply having a conversation with God: we listen, and we speak.

LIFELINE
To start getting balance in your life, start choosing to be content with who you are and with what you have.

Listening
Spend a few minutes simply being quiet. As you consider the ideas in today's reading—including the LifeLine—what thoughts does God bring to mind? You may get a sense that you are to start doing something—or stop doing something. Perhaps you will recognize some changes that might be good to make.

Talking
Speak to God as if He is sitting right next to you—and use the everyday words you would use if you were talking to a friend. Thank God for what He has taught you about your use of time. Ask Him to help you use what you've learned. One of these may help you get started:

Lord, forgive me for not being content with certain things in my life and certain things about myself.

Show me why I'm living at the pace I'm living.

THE WEEK IN REVIEW

Learn to say no to the good, the worthwhile, and the useful so that you are free to say yes to the best.

▸

Don't let yourself get sidetracked by things that don't matter. You have one life. Invest it well.

▸

We are wise to frequently and regularly obey His command "Be still, and know that I am God" (Psalm 46:10).

▸

Don't promise without pondering. Don't decide without deliberating. Make commitments carefully.

▸

To start getting balance in your life, start choosing to be content with who you are and with what you have.

For Personal Reflection or Group Discussion

The plate-spinner exhausted himself by running back and forth to make sure none of his plates stopped spinning, fell, and shattered. You, too, may be exhausted from trying to keep all your plates spinning. Why do we tend to keep so many plates spinning? Consider the culture's message, one's personality, family pressure, legitimate needs, a force of habit, etc.

What are some benefits we might experience if we weren't juggling so many plates?

And what are some benefits we might experience if we were getting more rest? What keeps us—what keeps you—from saying no to busyness and yes to rest? What can people do to remove obstacles like those you identified?

Only two things that will last forever: God's Word and people. What are some specific ways you can invest in God's Word? What are some specific ways we can invest in people?

Why does having balance in our lives help us choose contentment?

Why are solid LifeLines that protect our time important? More specifically, what positive impact does establishing and maintaining strong LifeLines for our time have on our faith? our relationships? our health? our work?

1

SPIRITUAL HEALTH

WHICH PART OF THE ROPE?

Imagine a rope a couple of feet long that represents your life into eternity. A very small part of the rope—about 1 inch—is painted red, and that section represents your life on Earth. We live those years on Earth more stressed than blessed, obsessing on the red part of the rope, we live with no regard for eternity.

What does that kind of living look like? "I want to feel successful now." "During this little chunk of time in all eternity, I will work long hours so I can travel wherever I want to travel and eat at the best restaurants." Or "Yes, I work a lot of weekends, but I'm making good money and saving it all so that my kids won't have to take care of me in my retirement."

What will this approach to life mean in the future? The sobering truth is that everything you and I do in the present is either going to bring us to reward or regret. And what we do during that red part of the rope impacts what we will do during the eternity part.

> **EVERYTHING YOU AND I DO IN THE PRESENT IS EITHER GOING TO BRING US TO REWARD OR REGRET.**

People may look at some of your decisions and say, "You're crazy!" In fact, this happened to me when I started Rock Creek. I had people thinking I had lost my mind. After all, I had a good job at a great church, and some folks couldn't fathom my walking away from that to something that was nothing more than a dream. A few of these people were related to me, and others just knew my name, but they all felt like they knew what God wanted for me better than I knew.

Now, 23 years and thousands of people later, it's easy for people to say, "Wow! What a great decision that was!"

My point is this: in moments of spiritual stress, there will always be voices in your life trying to control your direction. Don't let them! Remember that the real craziness is living only for the red part of the rope rather than with an awareness of eternity.

We need to stop living just for the red part of the rope. Ignoring our spirit and its eternal future causes spiritual stress because we human beings are—first and foremost—spiritual beings. When we ignore that fact, we put spiritual stress on ourselves. This happens especially when we make bad decisions. Whenever I've made a decision based on my feelings rather than my faith, I experience spiritual stress. I've learned—the hard way—that my feelings tend to get in the way of God's direction. So now when I have to make a decision, I list my feelings about this decision, and then I list the aspects of the decision that requires faith. Doing so helps me clearly see what should drive my decision—and helps me avoid spiritual stress.

> **WHENEVER I'VE MADE A DECISION BASED ON MY FEELINGS RATHER THAN MY FAITH, I EXPERIENCE SPIRITUAL STRESS.**

Yet most of the time when we talk about stress, we address the red-rope matters of being too busy, not having enough time, struggling in a relationship, dealing with money problems, and worrying—and these are very real issues that we must attend to. But you and I need to face a certain spiritual issue in order to move from stressed to blessed.

Simply put, Satan wants to stress us out spiritually. That's why he tempts us to do things that contradict what we believe and what we know God's Word to say. We can become too self-confident or prideful, too distracted by the temptations of the world, the flesh, and the devil, and too busy fueling our insatiable ego with too many commitments, and our relationship with God is no longer the focal point of our lives. With our weakened beliefs, exhausting pace, and relentless busyness, we lose sight of eternity.

Satan used these same weapons against the Old Testament strongman named Samson. He had everything going for him—good looks, position, strength, God's blessing—but, spiritually, he was a moral wimp. Life went well for Samson early on, but somewhere along the way, he got sidetracked. He ended up blind and broken, emptied of his physical strength and being blessed at the last moment with the last of his spiritual strength. When he strayed from God's path, Samson lost his spiritual strength.

Keeping focused on eternity—rather than the red fraction of an inch—keeps us spiritually strong.

LIFELINE
Stop living just for the red part of the rope.

DIGGING DEEPER

LIFELINE
Stop living just for the red part of the rope.

We fix our eyes not on what is seen, but on what is unseen since what is seen is temporary, but what is unseen is eternal.
2 CORINTHIANS 4:18

Whoever sows to please their flesh, from the flesh will reap destruction; whoever sows to please the Spirit, from the Spirit will reap eternal life.
GALATIANS 6:8

Fight the good fight of the faith. Take hold of the eternal life to which you were called.
1 TIMOTHY 6:12

Below, write down any ideas prompted by either these verses or the following questions...

Describe your understanding of spiritual health before you read this devotional and after. What is one new thought or helpful reminder it provided?

What do you find most distracting about the red segment of the rope? What could you do to transform those distractions into pointers toward the eternal?

Why can a lesser focus on the red help you "fight the good fight of the faith"?

IN REAL LIFE

Two thousand years ago the apostle James wrote, "Be doers of the word, and not hearers only" (1:22). Reading and understanding the Bible is good, but it's not enough. We also need to put into action what we read. We need to be "doers of the word."

What idea from today's reading seems to be just for you?

What will you do in response to that insight? Be specific.

TALK IT THROUGH

We tend to make prayer more complicated than it needs to be. Prayer is simply having a conversation with God: we listen, and we speak.

LIFELINE
Stop living just for the red part of the rope.

Listening
Spend a few minutes simply being quiet. As you consider the ideas in today's reading—including the LifeLine—what thoughts does God bring to mind? You may get a sense that you are to start doing something—or stop doing something. Perhaps you will recognize some changes that might be good to make.

Talking
Speak to God as if He is sitting right next to you—and use the everyday words you would use if you were talking to a friend. Thank God for what He has taught you about spiritual health. Ask Him to help you use what you've learned. One of these may help you get started:

Please show me specific ways I am endangering my spiritual health.

Sensitize me to notice when I'm too focused on the red so I can focus anew on You and eternity.

2

SPIRITUAL HEALTH

SPIRITUAL SOLUTIONS FOR SPIRITUAL STRESS

The *Chicago Tribune* published a story about a man, going for a walk, who decided to take a shortcut across the Tri-State Freeway. After he managed to get to the middle of the freeway, his hat blew off. When he reached back for it, he was struck by oncoming traffic and instantly killed. The article ended with this sentence: "It's amazing how you can lose everything chasing nothing."

Have you ever stopped to think about what it is you're chasing in life—and the price you're paying for it? It's far too easy to get caught up in meaningless pursuits. We struggle to stay focused on what really matters. We find ourselves distracted by what's not important. We get sucked into Facebook or a TV show. We allow ourselves to get too involved in worries, wasting massive amounts of time and emotional energy on the game of "What If?"; in riches, coveting or chasing things we don't need; and in pleasures, succumbing to the desires of the moment rather than the long-term and eternal.

Samson, too, struggled to focus on the eternal and, specifically, on God's call to him to live according to a higher standard. Samson chose a lifestyle that created spiritual stress by distracting him from eternity and that ultimately drained him of his once-renown spiritual strength. We can learn from the three things that wrecked Samson's life.

First, avoid being self-indulgent. As we see in Samson's life, that path leads nowhere good. Our culture, however, encourages undisciplined lifestyles and being governed by our feelings. Even good things like food, money, sex, and sleep can be harmful if they are misused.

As we see in Judges 14–16, Samson's problem was lust. In three chapters, he has three different women. At the beginning of Judges 14, we read the following:

> *Samson went down to Timnah and saw there a young Philistine woman. When he returned, he said to his father and mother, "I have seen a Philistine woman in Timnah; now get her for me as my wife."*
>
> *His father and mother replied, "Isn't there an acceptable woman among your relatives or among all our people? Must you go to the uncircumcised Philistines to get a wife?"*
>
> *But Samson said to his father, "Get her for me. She's the right one for me." (v. 1–3)*

Samson was pleased by the Philistine woman when he looked at her, and that was his first mistake. He made a decision based on pleasure rather than God's instructions. We must make God-honoring decisions based on His principles rather than pleasure.

If we don't look to principles for guidance, we easily fall into self-indulgence. We do the fun thing, the convenient thing, but not necessarily the right thing.

God said to Samson, "Don't do it." His parents warned him. But he saw this woman, and his convictions vanished. Samson ignored God's plan and followed his feelings. The apostle Paul offered this commentary on such decisions: "You can't ignore God and get away with it: a man will always reap

> **IF WE DON'T LOOK TO PRINCIPLES FOR GUIDANCE, WE EASILY FALL INTO SELF-INDULGENCE.**

just the kind of crop he sows!" (Galatians 6:7 TLB). Peter agreed: "Live the rest of your earthly lives controlled by God's will and not by human desires" (1Peter 4:2 GNT).

To reduce spiritual stress, discipline your desires. Just because you want something doesn't mean you should have it.

In addition to showing us the danger of self-indulgence, Samson's life cautions us to avoid resentment. One reason is that resentment fuels anger and Samson lived on anger. He reacted violently to everything, and his primary motivation in life was to get even. In Judges 15:3, for instance, he claimed, "I have a right to get even with the Philistines; I will really harm them." When the Philistines killed his wife—after he set their crops on fire—Samson declared, "Since you've acted like this, I swear that I won't stop until I get my revenge on you" (v. 7).

Resentment leads people to react to circumstances rather than to act with wisdom. Resentment wastes time and energy. Resentment builds up inside and will, at some point, explode. No wonder resentment is always self-defeating. As two of Job's friends said, "To worry yourself to death with resentment would be a foolish, senseless thing to do" (Job 5:2 GNT) and "You are only hurting yourself with your anger!" (18:4 GNT). Solomon added, "A fool gives full vent to his anger, but a wise man holds it in check" (Proverbs 29:11 HCSB).

To reduce spiritual stress, restrain your reactions.

LIFELINE

Make God-honoring decisions based on His principles rather than pleasure. Discipline your desires. Restrain your reactions.

DIGGING DEEPER

LIFELINE
Make God-honoring decisions based on His principles rather than pleasure. Discipline your desires. Restrain your reactions.

"Seek first [God's] kingdom and his righteousness, and all these things [clothes and food] will be given to you as well."
JESUS IN MATTHEW 6:33

[The grace of God] teaches us to say "No" to ungodliness and worldly passions, and to live self-controlled, upright and godly lives in this present age.
TITUS 2:12

Live the rest of your earthly lives controlled by God's will and not by human desires.
1 PETER 4:2 GNT

Below, write down any ideas prompted by either these verses or the following questions...

___

___

___

___

___

___

What consequences have you experienced as a result of acting on pleasure rather than principle, of following your desires rather than disciplining them, and/or of letting your reactions gain dominance over good sense?

Why can daily spiritual disciplines, regular Christian practices, and/or relationships with fellow believers help you both make decisions according to God's principles and control your desires? If these disciplines, practices, or relationships are lacking in your life, what will you do to fill in those holes?

Which do you struggle most to control: your love of pleasure, ungodly desires, or unrestrained reactions? What can you do to find strength for those struggles?

IN REAL LIFE

Two thousand years ago the apostle James wrote, "Be doers of the word, and not hearers only" (1:22). Reading and understanding the Bible is good, but it's not enough. We also need to put into action what we read. We need to be "doers of the word."

What idea from today's reading seems to be just for you?

What will you do in response to that insight? Be specific.

TALK IT THROUGH

We tend to make prayer more complicated than it needs to be. Prayer is simply having a conversation with God: we listen, and we speak.

LIFELINE
Make God-honoring decisions based on His principles rather than pleasure. Discipline your desires. Restrain your reactions.

Listening
Spend a few minutes simply being quiet. As you consider the ideas in today's reading—including the LifeLine—what thoughts does God bring to mind? You may get a sense that you are to start doing something—or stop doing something. Perhaps you will recognize some changes that might be good to make.

Talking
Speak to God as if He is sitting right next to you—and use the everyday words you would use if you were talking to a friend. Thank God for what He has taught you about spiritual health. Ask Him to help you use what you've learned. One of these may help you get started:

Lord, I want to better know Your principles so that they guide my decisions and actions.

Please show me when and even why I am so undisciplined when it comes to controlling my desires and/or when and why my reactions so easily get out of hand—and what I can do to change.

3

SPIRITUAL HEALTH

KEEPING YOUR SPIRITUAL COMMITMENTS

A while back the *Denver Post* ran an article about a Montana sheep rancher who had tried just about everything—electric fences, odor sprays, loud radios, even sleeping in the sheep pen at night—to stop crafty coyotes from killing her sheep. In a single year she lost fifty newborn lambs—and then she discovered llamas.

These odd, funny-looking animals are afraid of nothing. "When llamas see something," she explained, "they put their head up and walk straight toward it.... Coyotes are opportunists, and llamas take that opportunity away."

The devil is also an opportunist far craftier than any coyote, and we need to resist him so that he will flee just as the coyotes flee when the llama approaches. He can tempt us—often quite subtly—to be less careful about our health, our money, and our commitments.

Samson made some commitments to God, and Samson's strength depended on his keeping those commitments. Early in his life, Samson took the Nazarite vow, thereby saying, "I belong 100% to God. I'm going to dedicate all my time, energy, and effort to God's work."

As a Nazarite, Samson was to never drink alcohol, never eat grapes, and never cut his hair. Samson's faithfulness to these requirements was key to his strength. Yet, as we see in Judges 16, Samson got careless and, smitten by Delilah, compromised his convictions.

Delilah was a knockout, and Samson fell in love. When Samson's enemies learned that Delilah was his girlfriend, they hired her to find out the secret of his strength. So every night she would woo Samson into telling her his secret. Playing along, Samson gave her false answers—until he didn't.

The first time Samson said, "If anyone ties me with seven fresh bowstrings that have not been dried, I'll become as weak as any other man" (Judges 16:7). When Delilah awakened him the next morning, he was tied with seven bowstrings and saw strangers in the room ready to take him. But Samson snapped the strings, beat up the guys, and threw them out.

The next night Delilah asked Samson the secret of his strength, and this time he said being tied with new ropes would drain his strength. When Delilah awakened him the next morning, he was bound with new rope and saw strangers in the room ready to take him. But Samson snapped the ropes, beat up the guys, and threw them out.

(You'd think Samson would figure out Delilah is up to no good. I guess Samson's elevator didn't go all the way to the top! This guy is not too smart.)

On the third night, Delilah asked Samson his secret, and this strong man said that braided hair would make him weak. He was getting closer to the truth, apparently still thinking he could handle the situation. When Delilah awakened him the next morning, his hair was braided, and he saw strangers in the room ready to take him. But Samson still had his strength. He bloodied a few more noses and tossed the guys out.

> **BUT SAMSON FINALLY GAVE IN.**

But Samson finally gave in. His lifestyle of self-indulgence, resentment, and carelessness caught up with him, Delilah's nagging—" she prodded him day after day until he was sick to death of it"—finally overcame him, and "he told her everything" (v. 17). A tragic statement!

Perhaps Samson fell for a setup Satan still uses today. Our enemy lets us think, "It will be different for me. I can handle it."

Well-respected leaders in government, politics, and business have thought that—and found themselves at the heart of widely publicized scandals. They have been careless about their commitments (perhaps abandoning basic ones like going to church, reading the Bible, and praying). Theirs was a gradual slide rather than a dramatic falling away, a slide resulting from making choices inconsistent with their long-held values. Too often the slide is abruptly stopped when these leaders are revealed, and they lose their marriage, family, position, reputation, and good name.

To reduce spiritual stress and protect your spiritual health, keep your commitments even when you just don't feel like it, you don't even want to, or you're tempted not to.

Beware of the slippery slope of self-indulgence, resentment, and carelessness.

And when it comes to dealing with temptation, we can learn a thing or two from the llama.

LIFELINE
"Resist the devil, and he will flee from you" (James 4:7). Be a llama.

DIGGING DEEPER

LIFELINE
"Resist the devil, and he will flee from you" (James 4:7). Be a llama.

Blessed is the one who does not walk in step with the wicked or stand in the way that sinners take or sit in the company of mockers.
PSALM 1:1

No temptation has overtaken you except what is common to mankind. And God is faithful; he will not let you be tempted beyond what you can bear. But when you are tempted, he will also provide a way out so that you can endure it.
1 CORINTHIANS 10:13

Be alert and of sober mind. Your enemy the devil prowls around like a roaring lion looking for someone to devour.
1 PETER 5:8

Below, write down any ideas prompted by either these verses or the following questions...

What does "Make the decision before you need to make the decision" mean in the context of this discussion of temptation?

What friends or activities seem to lead you into temptation? What friends and practices help you stand strong against temptation? What kind of friend or influence are you?

What encouragement to be a llama do you find in 1 Corinthians 10:13?

IN REAL LIFE

Two thousand years ago the apostle James wrote, "Be doers of the word, and not hearers only" (1:22). Reading and understanding the Bible is good, but it's not enough. We also need to put into action what we read. We need to be "doers of the word."

What idea from today's reading seems to be just for you?

What will you do in response to that insight? Be specific.

TALK IT THROUGH

We tend to make prayer more complicated than it needs to be. Prayer is simply having a conversation with God: we listen, and we speak.

LIFELINE
"Resist the devil, and he will flee from you" (James 4:7). Be a llama.

Listening
Spend a few minutes simply being quiet. As you consider the ideas in today's reading—including the LifeLine—what thoughts does God bring to mind? You may get a sense that you are to start doing something—or stop doing something. Perhaps you will recognize some changes that might be good to make.

Talking
Speak to God as if He is sitting right next to you—and use the everyday words you would use if you were talking to a friend. Thank God for what He has taught you about spiritual health. Ask Him to help you use what you've learned. One of these may help you get started:

Forgive me for the times this week when I freely entered a place where I knew temptation would hit hard and/or the times I did not call on Your power to help me stand strong against temptation.

Teach me to better recognize the deceiver's voice and therefore know to call on You to help me resist him.

SPIRITUAL HEALTH

PHYSICAL HEALTH, SPIRITUAL SIGNIFICANCE

T*wo raw eggs—and lots of cookies—daily.*
Three bottles of beer and a glass of whiskey.
Not drinking or smoking and getting plenty of sleep.
A bowl of oatmeal with fruit and five to seven pushups every morning.
Bacon, eggs, and grits for breakfast every day.
Never wearing makeup.
Good genes, some luck, a lot of ice cream, and never eating anything healthy.
Getting eight hours of sleep every night—and eating a lot of sushi.
No men—but plenty of exercise.

What you just read are the secrets to longevity shared by people who lived more than 100 years. Some items mentioned in this Health.com list are more surprising than others. Some are more typically known to contribute to good health. And good health matters not only to everyone on the planet but also to the One who created us. God wants you to be healthy.

Our Creator God also calls us to "honor God with your body" (1 Corinthians 6:20). What does that mean? It means that you are to take care of your body and use it for God's glory. That's how you honor Him.

In Romans 12:1 we read this command: "Offer your bodies as a living sacrifice, holy and pleasing to God—this is your true and proper worship." Some of us may need an attitude adjustment before we are able to think of our bodies as a potential sacrifice to the Lord! In other words, you may need to develop a healthier attitude toward your body. Specifically, you need to eliminate from your mind at least these three unhealthy attitudes, three unhealthy ways you think about your body.

First, don't reject your body—and I know that some of you are doing this. You want to send it back! "It's a mistake, God! You messed up."

Don't work to perfect your body. This is the opposite extreme. People who do this are always working toward total perfection. They worship and idolize their body.

Finally, don't neglect your body. Ignoring your health leads nowhere good.

Now, having identified unhealthy attitudes, consider these better replacement thoughts. First, believe the truth of Psalm 139:14—"I am fearfully and wonderfully made." Then, in light of that truth, respect and protect your body. And that may require you to make some changes. You see, God wants you to be healthy, but He also expects you to take an active role in getting and staying healthy. He has given you some responsibilities when it comes to taking care of your body. He expects you to follow His guidelines and make any necessary changes in your attitudes and actions. But first the what's-in-it-for-me question: Why change?

> "I AM FEARFULLY AND WONDERFULLY MADE."

Because...

You'll feel better if you take care of yourself.

And if you feel better, you'll look better.

You'll also live longer. Many studies show that people in good physical condition live longer.

There are also spiritual reasons for taking care of our bodies. First, it's an act of respect for our Creator. God made your body, a fact David praised in Psalm 139:13: "You created my inmost being; you knit me together in my mother's womb." What God creates, we should not destroy. God made your body and mine, so we should take care of them.

Jesus paid for your body. When Jesus died on the cross, He paid the price to redeem your soul from eternal destruction. As He paid for your soul, He also paid for your body. In other words, Jesus owns your body; it is on loan to you. We are wise to take good care of something we are borrowing!

The Holy Spirit lives in your body. If you are a Christian, the Bible says, be aware that "you yourselves are God's temple and that God's Spirit dwells in your midst" (1 Corinthians 3:16).

So why take care of your body? Because God made your body, Jesus died for your body, and the Holy Spirit lives in your body. It is only right, then, that we do the best we can to make our bodies worthy temples.

Even the people in first-century Corinth needed to be encouraged along these same lines. Paul wrote in 1 Corinthians 6:19–20, "Do you not know that your bodies are temples of the Holy Spirit, who is in you, whom you have received from God? You are not your own; you were bought at a price. Therefore honor God with your bodies."

LIFELINE

Take care of your body because God made your body, Jesus died for your body, and the Holy Spirit lives in your body.

DIGGING DEEPER

LIFELINE
Take care of your body because God made your body, Jesus died for your body, and the Holy Spirit lives in your body.

You knit me together in my mother's womb.
PSALM 139:13

[Pilate] had Jesus flogged, and handed him over to be crucified.... And they crucified him. At noon, darkness came over the whole land until three in the afternoon. And at three in the afternoon, Jesus cried out in a loud voice, "Eloi, Eloi, lema sabachthani?" (which means "My God, my God, why have you forsaken me?").
MARK 15:15, 24, 33-34

All of them were filled with the Holy Spirit.
ACTS 2:4

Below, write down any ideas prompted by either these verses or the following questions...

Which are you most tempted to do with your body: reject it, try to perfect it, or neglect it? What is one specific step you could take to move toward protecting and respecting your body?

Comment not only on Jesus' physical pain of the crucifixion but also on the emotional, relational, and spiritual pain of those last days and hours of His life on earth.

When have you been especially aware of the Holy Spirit's presence within you? Give an example or two.

IN REAL LIFE

Two thousand years ago the apostle James wrote, "Be doers of the word, and not hearers only" (1:22). Reading and understanding the Bible is good, but it's not enough. We also need to put into action what we read. We need to be "doers of the word."

What idea from today's reading seems to be just for you?

What will you do in response to that insight? Be specific.

TALK IT THROUGH

We tend to make prayer more complicated than it needs to be. Prayer is simply having a conversation with God: we listen, and we speak.

LIFELINE
Take care of your body because God made your body, Jesus died for your body, and the Holy Spirit lives in your body.

Listening
Spend a few minutes simply being quiet. As you consider the ideas in today's reading—including the LifeLine—what thoughts does God bring to mind? You may get a sense that you are to start doing something—or stop doing something. Perhaps you will recognize some changes that might be good to make.

Talking
Speak to God as if He is sitting right next to you—and use the everyday words you would use if you were talking to a friend. Thank God for what He has taught you about spiritual health. Ask Him to help you use what you've learned. One of these may help you get started:

Forgive me for rejecting my body, seeking to perfect my body, and/or neglecting my body, which is a temple of Your Holy Spirit.

Holy Spirit, I ask You to give me the self-control I need to exercise regularly and effectively.

5

SPIRITUAL HEALTH

THE HEALTH OF OUR WHOLE BEING

Lord, grant me the strength that I may not fall
Into the clutches of cholesterol....
Teach me the evils of Hollandaise,
Of pasta and gobs of mayonnaise.
And crisp fried chicken from the South.
Lord, if You love me, shut my mouth.
VICTOR BUONO

We've been looking at spiritual health, but in scripture, God addresses the health of our whole being—spiritual, emotional, and physical. That means, when you follow the principles of God's Word, you're going to be a healthier person. Let's look at five biblical principles for building a healthy body.

1. Maintain your ideal weight. Science supports the fact that each of us has an ideal weight based on bone structure and height. Research, however, shows that 50 million Americans are overweight. (Case in point: the 1976 Yankee Stadium lost 4,000 seats because the 18-inch seats were replaced by 22-inch seats!) We cannot eat everything we want and still maintain our ideal weight. First Thessalonians 4:4 speaks to that issue: "Each of you should learn to control his own body in a way that is holy and honorable." We can learn the self-discipline that's necessary for maintaining an ideal weight.

2. Balance your diet. Eating is not an end in itself. We eat to live; we don't live to eat. So we need to control the quality and the quantity of what we eat. We need to balance both what we eat and how much we eat, and the Bible is full of such nutritional advice. Proverbs 25:27 states, "It is not good to eat too much honey" (read: sugar). Leviticus 3:17 offers this warning to God's people: "You must not eat any fat"—and that was written BC. Before Cholesterol! God knew that animal fat raises our cholesterol. Such nutritional advice, sprinkled throughout the scriptures, still holds true today.

3. Decide on a regular exercise program. How do you know you're out of shape? When you feel like the morning after, and you didn't go anywhere the night before. Or when your knees buckle but your belt won't.

In 1 Timothy 4:8 we find something we already know: "Physical exercise has some value" (GNT). We all understand that God designed our bodies to be active and that exercise is good for us. But exercise is no longer built into our days. Two thousand years ago everyone did physical labor; not many of us do so today. Two thousand years ago people walked everywhere; we have cars. Two thousand years ago people ate natural foods; we eat processed food and junk food.

> **GOD DESIGNED OUR BODIES TO BE ACTIVE AND THAT EXERCISE IS GOOD FOR US.**

And these are some of the reasons we need to commit to a regular exercise program. And what is the most common excuse for not doing so? "I don't have time!" Do you have time to be sick? If you don't exercise, you'll probably find time to be sick! So how do you want to spend your time?

4. Get enough sleep and rest. Psalm 127:2 says that God "grants peace to those he loves" or, as the Living Bible puts it, "God wants His loved ones to get their rest." Since I've started taking a day off, I'm amazed how much better I feel. Jesus insisted that His disciples take some time off: "The apostles gathered around Jesus and reported to him all they had done and taught. Then, because so many people were coming and going that they did not even have a chance to eat, he said to them, 'Come with me by yourselves to a quiet place and get some rest'" (Mark 6:30–31). Planned vacations, adequate sleep, regular downtime—all of this is vital to your physical health.

5. Live in peace with God. As Proverbs 14:30 says, "A heart at peace gives life to the body." Our emotions have a big effect on our physical health just as our physical health has a tremendous effect on our emotions. You cannot fill your life with guilt, worry, bitterness, and anger and also be in great health.

Physical health comes when you take care of your body, mind, and soul; when you pay attention to the emotional and spiritual dimensions of your life as well as the physical.

In fact, did you know that salvation means "wholeness"? The first step toward being physically, emotionally, spiritually, mentally, and socially whole is to ask Jesus Christ to be Lord your life and say, "Jesus, help me get it together in every area of my life." And He will.

LIFELINE
A balanced diet, regular exercise, enough sleep and rest, and living at peace with God lead to the health of our whole being— spiritual, emotional, and physical.

DIGGING DEEPER

LIFELINE
A balanced diet, regular exercise, enough sleep and rest, and living at peace with God lead to the health of our whole being—spiritual, emotional, and physical.

*In vain you rise early
and stay up late,
toiling for food to eat—
for he grants sleep to those he loves.*
PSALM 127:2

God demonstrates his own love for us in this: While we were still sinners, Christ died for us.
ROMANS 8:8

The fruit of the Spirit is love, joy, peace, forbearance, kindness, goodness, faithfulness, gentleness, and self-control.
GALATIANS 5:22-23

Below, write down any ideas prompted by either these verses or the following questions...

_____
_____
_____
_____
_____

Which aspect of your health—eating a balanced diet, exercising regularly, getting enough sleep and rest, and living at peace with God—do you struggle with most? Why might that be the case? What might you do to overcome that struggle and/or remove that barrier?

What does it mean to you to live at peace with God? What would you say to explain the concept to a nonbeliever?

Why is self-control essential to maintaining spiritual, emotional, and physical health? What might you do to strengthen your self-control?

IN REAL LIFE

Two thousand years ago the apostle James wrote, "Be doers of the word, and not hearers only" (1:22). Reading and understanding the Bible is good, but it's not enough. We also need to put into action what we read. We need to be "doers of the word."

What idea from today's reading seems to be just for you?

What will you do in response to that insight? Be specific.

TALK IT THROUGH

We tend to make prayer more complicated than it needs to be. Prayer is simply having a conversation with God: we listen, and we speak.

LIFELINE
A balanced diet, regular exercise, enough sleep and rest, and living at peace with God lead to the health of our whole being—spiritual, emotional, and physical.

Listening
Spend a few minutes simply being quiet. As you consider the ideas in today's reading—including the LifeLine—what thoughts does God bring to mind? You may get a sense that you are to start doing something—or stop doing something. Perhaps you will recognize some changes that might be good to make.

Talking
Speak to God as if He is sitting right next to you—and use the everyday words you would use if you were talking to a friend. Thank God for what He has taught you about spiritual health. Ask Him to help you use what you've learned. One of these may help you get started:

You know how weary I am and how I struggle to get enough sleep. I ask for both the grace of sleep and the grace of entrusting all my cares and concerns and those I love to Your good and perfect care.

Help me as I address each component of life so that I may indeed honor you with my well-fed, well-exercised, and well-rested body.

THE WEEK IN REVIEW

⇐ LIFELINES ⇒
for Spiritual Health

Stop living just for the red part of the rope.

▸

Make God-honoring decisions based on His principles rather than pleasure. Discipline your desires. Restrain your reactions.

▸

"Resist the devil, and he will flee from you" (James 4:7). Be a llama.

▸

Take care of your body because God made your body, Jesus died for your body, and the Holy Spirit lives in your body.

▸

A balanced diet, regular exercise, enough sleep and rest, and living at peace with God lead to the health of our whole being—spiritual, emotional, and physical.

For Personal Reflection or Group Discussion

What do you find most helpful about the rope metaphor? What are you doing—what can you do—to stay focused on the rope when the demands of the red inch are very real and ever-present?

As I mentioned, when I have to make a decision, I list my feelings about the decision, and then I list the aspects of the decision that requires faith. Doing so helps me clearly see what should drive my decision. What do you see as the value of this approach? The challenge? The benefits? For what decision you face will you make this kind of list?

A coach was fond of reminding his team that it's not always easy to do what's right, as Samson's life illustrates all too well. What do you do to find strength when you're struggling to do what is right? What support and reinforcements do you turn to—or will you turn to next time?

Samson teaches us to protect our spiritual health by keeping our commitments to God even when we don't feel like it, we don't want to, or we're tempted not to. What would you say are your commitments to Jesus? Be specific. Talking about these commitments and/or putting them down on paper can help you clarify what your life is about and—when necessary—help you, like a llama, stand up against the devil.

What was the most important takeaway from "Physical Health, Spiritual Significance"? Why? What change(s) in your attitude and/or your actions have you already made?

As 1 Timothy 4:8 points out, spiritual exercise is more important than physical exercise, and we need to attend to both. What is your spiritual exercise program? Your physical exercise program? What would you like to do to strengthen each?

1

WORK

THE CAUSE AND CONSEQUENCES OF BURNOUT

I've always heard it said, "Do what you love and you'll never work a day in your life!"

Well, for me that simply isn't true.

I absolutely love what I do, which is what I believe God wants me to do, and I have trouble setting boundaries. I find myself saying yes to too many things, and I get burned out.

You see, I am a recovering workaholic. I have to really work at not working. You may be just like me. There is always work to do, isn't there? And because of all the ways we have to communicate in today's world, we feel we should always produce.

Also, early in my life I quickly learned that the way up the ladder at any job was to outwork everyone else. And, frankly, in some jobs I've have had, that was pretty easy. Today we're seeing that a solid work ethic is a dying value, but I had to learn the difference between a work ethic and a healthy work ethic.

So along the way, I have burned out a few times, but Elijah's story has always helped me get out of the darkness that burnout brings.

When we first saw a burned-out Elijah, he was emotionally distraught, feeling like he had no control over his life, and not seeing reality clearly. The evil Queen Jezebel wanted him killed, and that death threat contributed to Elijah's fear, resentment, low self-esteem, anger, loneliness, and worry. To his burnout. And we see in Elijah some consequences of burnout:

First, burnout distorts our priorities because we give more weight to our feelings than to facts—and feelings can lie. Elijah, for instance, "prayed that he might die. 'I have had enough, LORD!'" (1 Kings 19:4). Despite God's showing up in a big way to demonstrate His superiority over the prophets of Baal (1 Kings 18 tells that great story), Elijah was ready to give up. Overwhelmed by emotions and exhaustion, he asked God to take his life.

> **"I HAVE HAD ENOUGH, LORD!"**

Burnout also damages our perspective, and we exaggerate the negative. We blow the negative out of proportion, often to the point of not being able to acknowledge any positive at all. We feel as if everything is going wrong. That was definitely Elijah's perspective: "I am the only [faithful] one left… now they are trying to kill me too" (v. 10). The prophet is having a pity party.

The truth is, only one person was fighting Elijah, and that person was Queen Jezebel. Having become jealous of Elijah's popularity and power, she sent to Elijah a messenger with this warning: "If you don't get out of the country, I'm going to have you killed within a few hours" (my paraphrase).

So Elijah ran across the desert to a cave where he hid and felt sorry for himself. Although only one person was against him, he cried out, "Everybody's against me!"

If Elijah had really thought about the situation—if he hadn't listened to his feelings but looked at the facts instead—he would have realized that if Jezebel really wanted to kill him, she would have sent a hitman, not a messenger. Furthermore, Jezebel knew that if she killed Elijah, she would make him a martyr and a hero to the people of Israel.

Acknowledging facts, not feelings, and choosing to trust God can change your perspective, grow your faith, and enable you to see life through God's eyes. In Elijah's case, he was able to see seven thousand faithful Israelites. He was not the only one left.

That said, burnout will cause you to exaggerate the negative, and that inaccurate perspective can lead us to blame ourselves for things that aren't our fault. In Elijah's case—when he has been doing everything a prophet is supposed to do but it isn't working—the self-blame makes sense. The only other One to blame would be God—and that wasn't happening!

So what is going on? It could be that you just aren't where God wants you to be, and He will allow burnout to get your attention, to perhaps knock you down emotionally and to readjust your perspective on life?. Because that's what burnout does.

Finally, burnout derails our pursuit of our God-given purpose. When we feel like failures, we too easily compare ourselves to the successful people around us. Actually, we compare our weaknesses to other people's strengths, and of course, our weaknesses become huge.

Don't go there! Remember, everybody is different—and only you can be you.

LIFELINE
Burnout distorts priorities, damages perspective and detrails purpose.

DIGGING DEEPER

LIFELINE
Burnout distorts priorities, damages perspective and detrails purpose.

Yes, my soul, find rest in God; my hope comes from him.

Truly he is my rock and my salvation; he is my fortress, I will not be shaken.
PSALM 62:5-6

Even youths grow tired and weary, and young men stumble and fall; but those who hope in the LORD will renew their strength.

They will soar on wings like eagles; they will run and not grow weary, they will walk and not be faint.
ISAIAH 40:30-31

"Come to me, all you who are weary and burdened, and I will give you rest. Take my yoke upon you and learn from me, for I am gentle and humble in heart, and you will find rest for your souls."
JESUS IN MATTHEW 11:28-29

Below, write down any ideas prompted by either these verses or the following questions...

What can fuel addiction to work? If you battle that tendency, what is fueling it? What are you doing—or could you be doing—to combat it?

Where, if at all, do you see yourself in today's description of burnout?

What action step might you take? Or when has this description of burnout fit you all too well? What did you do to recover?

IN REAL LIFE

Two thousand years ago the apostle James wrote, "Be doers of the word, and not hearers only" (1:22). Reading and understanding the Bible is good, but it's not enough. We also need to put into action what we read. We need to be "doers of the word."

What idea from today's reading seems to be just for you?

What will you do in response to that insight? Be specific.

TALK IT THROUGH

We tend to make prayer more complicated than it needs to be. Prayer is simply having a conversation with God: we listen, and we speak.

LIFELINE
Burnout distorts priorities, damages perspective and detrails purpose.

Listening
Spend a few minutes simply being quiet. As you consider the ideas in today's reading—including the LifeLine—what thoughts does God bring to mind? You may get a sense that you are to start doing something—or stop doing something. Perhaps you will recognize some changes that might be good to make.

Talking
Speak to God as if He is sitting right next to you—and use the everyday words you would use if you were talking to a friend. Thank God for what He has taught you about work and rest. Ask Him to help you use what you've learned. One of these may help you get started:

You know I tend more toward workaholism/laziness. Please help me understand why and especially how to be free of that tendency.

Thank You for the gift of rest and the ways You have used it to bless me.

2
WORK
FIRST AID FOR BURNOUT

So... how do you feel about your job? After all, the workplace—whether a paid position, volunteer work, or parenting full-time at home—may be the greatest contributor to burnout.

Each day in America 50,000 people who are receiving a paycheck for their work quit their jobs. And 85 percent of the people who don't say they could work harder at their job—if they wanted to.

Statistics about job satisfaction reveal that 10–20 percent of people who work love their job, and 10–20 percent hate their job. That means a large percent of the working population are coasting in the middle.

> **IF YOU ARE SLOGGING BUT WANT TO FEEL BETTER ABOUT YOUR JOB, YOU HAVE TO FIND WHAT YOU NEED TO FIX.**

If you are slogging but want to feel better about your job, you have to find what you need to fix. And—believe it or not—taking care of yourself physically may be the best first step. That's because of the complex interrelationship between our physical, mental, emotional, and spiritual health. So we shouldn't be surprised that the Creator of the human body addressed the physical needs of His discouraged prophet Elijah right away:

> *[Elijah] lay down under the bush and fell asleep.*
>
> *All at once an angel touched him and said, "Get up and eat." He looked around, and there by his head was a cake of bread baked over hot coals, and a jar of water. He ate and drank and then lay down again.*
>
> *The angel of the LORD came back a second time and touched him and said, "Get up and eat, for the journey is too much for you." So he got up and ate and drank. Strengthened by that food, he traveled forty days and forty nights until he reached Horeb, the mountain of God.*
>
> **(1 KINGS 19:5-8)**

When Elijah burned out, God didn't give him a lecture. God didn't scold him. God didn't say, "Remember what happened two days ago? The greatest victory of your whole life? Pull yourself together!" God didn't preach at Elijah or yell at him. Instead—perfect Father that He is—God graced Elijah with sleep and food.

God understands your body better than you do; God knows the value of sleep. In fact, sometimes the most spiritual thing you can do is sleep. I say that because when we're tired, you don't handle stress well or make good decisions. Never make a major decision when you're depressed or tired: it will almost always be wrong. Wait until you've been at least somewhat recharged by a good night's sleep. On occasion, a single good night's rest can completely transform your perspective on life.

> **GOD UNDERSTANDS YOUR BODY BETTER THAN YOU DO.**

After God tended to Elijah's physical needs, He gave His prophet the opportunity to vent emotionally—and we are wise to do the same. Whatever we're feeling, let's tell it to God. Pray about it. Let go of it. Complain a bit and confess to the Lord any sin that surfaces as you do so. Elijah didn't hold back: "I have been very zealous for the LORD God Almighty. The Israelites have rejected your covenant, broken down your altars, and put your prophets to death with the sword. I am the only one left, and now they are trying to kill me too" (v. 10).

When God invited Elijah to tell Him what he was thinking and feeling, Elijah did so: "There are six things that bug me, God. I'm afraid. I'm bitter. I'm angry. I'm lonely. I'm worried. And I'm depressed." Those six emotions churning inside are a sure recipe for burnout. Whenever you swallow your emotions, your stomach keeps score.

Knowing the value of this kind of openness and honesty, God let Elijah complain. Rather than interrupting Elijah or criticizing him, God listened—and He will do the same for you. He is not surprised when we complain.

Have you ever wondered why some of the psalms got into the Holy Bible? In some of the psalms he wrote, David was open, honest, and pretty vindictive: "God, I hate my enemies! I want to see them all dead and their whole families slaughtered." God allowed those psalms into His Word because David was being genuine and real with God… and that's what our heavenly Father wants from us. His love for us is unconditional. Never should our emotions keep us from going to Him and sharing all that we're thinking and feeling.

LIFELINE
First aid for burnout includes food, rest, and emotional venting.

DIGGING DEEPER

LIFELINE
First aid for burnout includes food, rest, and emotional venting.

Relieve the troubles of my heart and free me from my anguish.
PSALM 25:17

God wants his loved ones to get their proper rest.
PSALM 127:2 (TLB)

Because so many people were coming and going that they did not even have a chance to eat, he said to them, "Come with me by yourselves to a quiet place and get some rest."
JESUS TO HIS DISCIPLES IN MARK 6:31

Below, write down any ideas prompted by either these verses or the following questions...

Why is sleep sometimes the most spiritual thing you can do?

What, if anything, keeps you from being completely open with God about your thoughts and feelings? What lie are you believing—and needing to replace with truth?

Food, rest, emotional openness—which of these essentials do you most struggle to get enough of? Why?

IN REAL LIFE

Two thousand years ago the apostle James wrote, "Be doers of the word, and not hearers only" (1:22). Reading and understanding the Bible is good, but it's not enough. We also need to put into action what we read. We need to be "doers of the word."

What idea from today's reading seems to be just for you?

What will you do in response to that insight? Be specific.

TALK IT THROUGH

We tend to make prayer more complicated than it needs to be. Prayer is simply having a conversation with God: we listen, and we speak.

LIFELINE
First aid for burnout includes food, rest, and emotional venting.

Listening
Spend a few minutes simply being quiet. As you consider the ideas in today's reading—including the LifeLine—what thoughts does God bring to mind? You may get a sense that you are to start doing something—or stop doing something. Perhaps you will recognize some changes that might be good to make.

Talking
Speak to God as if He is sitting right next to you—and use the everyday words you would use if you were talking to a friend. Thank God for what He has taught you about work and rest. Ask Him to help you use what you've learned. One of these may help you get started:

Lord, I want to risk being more emotionally honest with You than I have ever been....

Help me to eat right and get enough rest so that I can be the person You created me to be and do the work You have prepared for me to do.

3
WORK
WHAT ARE YOU FOCUSED ON?

A pastor dies and goes to heaven. As he stands in line at the pearly gates, St. Peter asks the man in front of him, "Who are you?"

"I'm Jim Cohen, a taxi driver from New York City."

St. Peter says, "Welcome!" and gives him a gold staff and a bag of jewels. "Come on in!"

"Thank you!" says the cab driver.

The pastor then says to St. Peter, "I'm Jim Winters, and I was pastor at St. Luke's Cathedral in Grand Rapids."

Peter says, "Welcome!" and gives him a wooden staff and a bag of stones.

The pastor is stunned. "Wait! The cab driver got gold, and I—a pastor—got wood?"

"Up here," St. Peter explains, "we reward by results. When you preached, people slept. When he drove, people prayed!"

What kind of impact you are having on people in your workplace is a topic for another day. Right now consider whether you are allowing your workplace to push you closer to God or drive you further from Him. The direction you're moving depends on your focus. You can focus on what you can accomplish, or you can focus on what God can accomplish through you (a perspective that gives you eternal purpose at your workplace). You sharpen this focus when you choose to work not for a paycheck or a good performance review, but for the pleasure of your Audience of One.

Understanding the importance of working for Him instead of lesser reasons, God tended to Elijah's physical needs, gave him the opportunity to process his emotions, and then met his need for spiritual restoration after a climactic experience and the letdown that came with having a price on his head. After telling Elijah to stand on a mountaintop because "the LORD is about to pass by" (1 Kings 19:11), God put on quite a production to remind Elijah about the nature of the God he was serving:

> *A great and powerful wind tore the mountains apart and shattered the rocks before the LORD, but the LORD was not in the wind. After the wind, there was an earthquake, but the LORD was not in the earthquake. After the earthquake came to a fire, but the LORD was not in the fire. After the fire came a gentle whisper. (v. 11-13)*

God put on quite a show, but He didn't speak to Elijah through the wind, earthquake, or fire. God spoke to Elijah in a whisper.

Why did God do this? To remind Elijah of His power. The unspoken message to Elijah and you and me was "I am sovereign. I am powerful and good and wise. When things look bad or are in fact bad, remember that My power is far greater than any problem you will face. I am in control." God was saying, "Focus on Me, not on your problem."

This message is key for someone suffering from burnout because the root of all burnout is playing God. When you play God—when you act as if God doesn't matter, you're in charge, and you can make life work—you set yourself up for burnout. God never meant for you to be the manager of your life; He rightfully wants to manage your life. After all, you were made by Him and for Him. Until you understand that basic truth, life isn't going to make sense.

WHEN YOU PLAY GOD—YOU SET YOURSELF UP FOR BURNOUT.

So God used this mountaintop moment to remind Elijah of His power as well as of the fact that He was right there with him, that He hadn't gone away. Maybe you need that reminder too. If so, make some time to just be quiet, get alone with God, and be honest with Him about your thoughts, your emotions, your life. Also, ask Him to show you—just as He told Elijah about the 7,000 faithful followers—that you are not alone.

When Elijah heard the Lord's gentle whisper, he was once again honest with God, and God restored him with the instruction "Go back the way you came" (v. 15). When God gives you direction and you accept His direction, spiritual restoration is the result. Spiritual restoration happens when we respond obediently to God's direction."

God can cure your burnout, but you have to listen for His voice and act on it.

LIFELINE
Focus on God, not on your problem.

DIGGING DEEPER

LIFELINE
Focus on God, not on your problem.

Focusing on the self is the opposite of focusing on God. Anyone completely absorbed in self ignores God, ends up thinking more about self than God. That person ignores who God is and what he is doing. And God isn't pleased with being ignored.
ROMANS 8:7-8 MSG

I want you woven into a tapestry of love, in touch with everything, there is to know of God. Then you will have minds confident and at rest, focused on Christ, God's great mystery.
COLOSSIANS 2:2 MSG

Let us run with perseverance the race marked out for us, fixing our eyes on Jesus, the pioneer, and perfecter of faith.
HEBREWS 12:1-2

Below, write down any ideas prompted by either these verses or the following questions...

When have you consciously keep your focus on God during a challenging season of life? What enabled you to do so, and what difference did that make?

What suggestions would you give to someone struggling to focus on God instead of his or her problem?

"What would it look like to "fix your eyes on Jesus" when encountering challenges at work?"

IN REAL LIFE

Two thousand years ago the apostle James wrote, "Be doers of the word, and not hearers only" (1:22). Reading and understanding the Bible is good, but it's not enough. We also need to put into action what we read. We need to be "doers of the word."

What idea from today's reading seems to be just for you?

What will you do in response to that insight? Be specific.

TALK IT THROUGH

We tend to make prayer more complicated than it needs to be. Prayer is simply having a conversation with God: we listen, and we speak.

LIFELINE
Focus on God, not on your problem.

Listening
Spend a few minutes simply being quiet. As you consider the ideas in today's reading—including the LifeLine—what thoughts does God bring to mind? You may get a sense that you are to start doing something—or stop doing something. Perhaps you will recognize some changes that might be good to make.

Talking
Speak to God as if He is sitting right next to you—and use the everyday words you would use if you were talking to a friend. Thank God for what He has taught you recovering from burnout. Ask Him to help you use what you've learned. One of these may help you get started:

I ask You to use my problems to keep me mindful that I need You, that I need to look to You always.

Teach me to keep my focus on You, however dark or overwhelming or impossible my circumstances look.

4

WORK

HOSTILE COWORKERS

Escape.

That word comes to my mind whenever I think about toxic coworkers. I just want to find some way to escape—and run! I confess I had that reaction to a coworker named John.

Driven by the deep desire to be on the "inside" and to be "somebody," John always took every opportunity to one-up the person in the room. If someone went on a vacation, John told about a better trip he and his family had taken. Whatever car his coworkers drove, or restaurant they ate at, or clothes they wore, John had done it better. His obnoxious attempts at one-upmanship were destroying the workplace. His desire to get ahead of others had led to one lie after another. What had been a great environment was now characterized by annoyance, tension, and even paranoia—all because of one person.

John had singlehandedly created a hostile workplace.

Maybe you work—or have worked—with a John. And maybe it won't surprise you at all to read that hostile coworkers are the number one source of stress at work. We all know hostile people, those men, and women who behave as if the rules of society simply don't apply to them.

It's absolutely imperative that you acknowledge who the hostile people are at work and know how to deal with them. They are dangerous to be around, so you need to beware.

Hostility can manifest in a variety of ways. People can display one or more of these characteristics:

Demanding—These very controlling, very intimidating individuals always want to be in charge.

Dishonest—Hostile people will lie to you, cheat you, stab you in the back, and betray you.

Disagreeable—They are chronic complainers, always negative, and always uncooperative.

Defensive—Being thin-skinned, hostile people take offense at everything you say. You have to walk on eggshells around them, or they're going to get their feelings hurt.

Demeaning—Very disrespectful and always critical, hostile coworkers treat you like dirt. Nothing you ever do is good.

What does the Bible say about dealing with hostile coworkers? We're going to look at three guidelines.

1) I can't please everyone, but "if it is possible, as far as it depends on you, live at peace with everyone" (Romans 12:18).

When it comes to relationships, you can only do what you can do. And in this case, accepting that you can't please a hostile coworker no matter how hard you try is an important step to take.

Equally important as understanding who at the office can never be pleased is knowing that you don't need to please everybody. Consider this ancient wisdom for that age-old issue: "It is dangerous to be concerned with what others think of you" (Proverbs 29:25 GNT).

Always worrying about what other people think about you is a trap. You do not have to be liked and approved of by everybody in

> **YOU DO NOT HAVE TO BE LIKED AND APPROVED OF BY EVERYBODY IN ORDER TO BE HAPPY.**

order to be happy. Simplify your life and live for your Audience of One just as Jesus did: "I only seek to please Him who sent me" (John 5:29 paraphrased). Not even Jesus tried to please everyone. He knew it wouldn't work.

2) I will not retaliate: "Do not repay evil with evil or insult with an insult" (1 Peter 3:9).

That's right: even when people take shots at you, refuse to retaliate. When that coworker stabs you in the back or takes credit for something you did, don't hit back. Again, we look to Proverbs for wisdom: "When a fool is annoyed, he quickly lets it be known. Smart people will ignore an insult" (12:16 GNT). A mark of Christian maturity is a controlled reaction, and often that controlled reaction is simply silence.

3) I must respond with love: "Love your enemies, bless them that curse you, do good to those who hate you and pray for those who despitefully use you" (Matthew 5:44 KJV).

Love is the bottom line. In spite of who they are and how they act, be who you are and act with Christian love. Don't let unhappy people change you! Instead, do as Jesus instructs: love them, bless them, do good to them, and pray for them. As the writer of Proverbs has observed, "When a man's ways are pleasing to the LORD, he makes even his enemies to be at peace with him" (Proverbs 16:7 ESV).

LIFELINE
When dealing with hostile workers, accept that you can't live at peace with everyone; don't retaliate, and always respond with love.

DIGGING DEEPER

LIFELINE
When dealing with hostile workers, accept that you can't live at peace with everyone; don't retaliate, and always respond with love.

"Love your enemies, bless them that curse you, do good to those who hate you and pray for those who despitefully use you."
JESUS IN MATTHEW 5:44 KJV

"Love your enemies, do good to those who hate you, bless those who curse you, pray for those who mistreat you.... If you love those who love you, what credit is that to you? Even sinners love those who love them."
JESUS IN LUKE 6:27-28, 32

If it is possible, as far as it depends on you, live at peace with everyone.
ROMANS 12:18

Below, write down any ideas prompted by either these verses or the following questions...

_____
_____
_____
_____
_____
_____

Review the characteristics of hostile people found in today's devotion. Which—if any—might characterize your behavior or attitude on occasion? What will you do to prevent it next time?

Look again at Romans 12:18 above. What relationships, if any, might God be giving you permission to step back—if not completely away—from? What do you appreciate about the opening "If it is possible"?

What divine call to action—call to bring peace to a relationship that needs healing—do you hear in Romans 12:18?

IN REAL LIFE

Two thousand years ago the apostle James wrote, "Be doers of the word, and not hearers only" (1:22). Reading and understanding the Bible is good, but it's not enough. We also need to put into action what we read. We need to be "doers of the word."

What idea from today's reading seems to be just for you?

What will you do in response to that insight? Be specific.

TALK IT THROUGH

We tend to make prayer more complicated than it needs to be. Prayer is simply having a conversation with God: we listen, and we speak.

LIFELINE
When dealing with hostile workers, accept that you can't live at peace with everyone; don't retaliate, and always respond with love.

Listening
Spend a few minutes simply being quiet. As you consider the ideas in today's reading—including the LifeLine—what thoughts does God bring to mind? You may get a sense that you are to start doing something—or stop doing something. Perhaps you will recognize some changes that might be good to make.

Talking
Speak to God as if He is sitting right next to you—and use the everyday words you would use if you were talking to a friend. Thank God for what He has taught you about dealing with hostile coworkers. Ask Him to help you use what you've learned. One of these may help you get started:

Help me to love the hard-to-love people in my life with my words and my actions.

Show me what good You would have me do for the hostile people in my life and please enable me to pray sincerely for them.

5

WORK

THE BURDEN OF UNREALISTIC EXPECTATIONS

He was a lifetime .300 hitter, National League MVP, and the winner of numerous Gold Glove Awards for his fielding.

In spite of his numerous awards and impressive stats, Keith Hernandez missed out on something that was critically important. Listen to what he said during a candid interview about his father:

> One day I asked my dad, "I have a lifetime .300 batting average. What more do you want?" My dad said, "But someday you're going to look back and say, 'I could have done more.'"

Not measuring up, never doing enough—that's the kind of pressure a lot of people live under, and maybe you're one of them. Are you always feeling like you could have done more or could do more now? That sense may come from a parent, a spouse, or, because of failures in your past, even yourself.

The workplace, the boss, and coworkers can also communicate this crippling message, making them, in a sense, your enemies. Learn from David that God is your best Defender:

> *You prepare a table before me in the presence of my enemies,*
> *and you anoint my head with oil; my cup overflows.*
> **PSALM 23:5**

Speaking metaphorically, David was saying that God is good, so good that He prepares a banquet for David in front of his enemies. This good God also anoints David's head with oil, an action that says to the world, "This is My guy, one I have chosen to lead My people! Back off!" As a result, David says, "My cup overflows with gratitude for God's goodness to me. I have critics, enemies, and attackers, but God keeps blessing me and blessing me and blessing me." No wonder David confidently proclaimed his trust in God:

> *I love you, LORD, my strength.*

> *The LORD is my rock, my fortress, and my deliverer;*
> *my God is my rock, in whom I take refuge,*
> *my shield and the horn of my salvation, my stronghold.*
> **PSALM 18:1-2 GNT**

But what does resting on these truths look like in a hostile work environment? When people criticize us unjustly, make false accusations, and say all kinds of mean things about us, we are wise to follow Jesus' example: after He was arrested, the chief priests and Sanhedrin demanded that He tell them if He was the Messiah, Son of God—and "Jesus remained silent" (Matthew 26:63). We are most like Christ when we remain silent in response to being attacked. We are most like Christ when we remain silent in response to being criticized.

> **WE ARE MOST LIKE CHRIST WHEN WE REMAIN SILENT.**

I'll tell you a little secret, and I've learned this from experience. If we choose to be silent when we are attacked or criticized, we often end up gaining power, authority, influence and anointing.

James 1:19 offers further guidance for dealing with critics and other difficult people in the workplace: "Everyone should be quick to listen, slow to speak, and slow to become angry." So, for instance, when you confront a hostile person at work, listen for that person's hurt. Why am I sure hostility reveals hurt? Because hurt people always hurt other people. And when you understand their hurt, even just a little bit, you'll better understand why they do the things they do. That understanding always brings patience.

Also, drawing close to the Good Shepherd as David did means having reassurance like this: "Surely goodness and love will follow me all the days of my life"(Psalm 23:6).

When a shepherd has a flock of sheep, he usually has a couple of sheepdogs. The shepherd leads from the front, and the sheepdogs are at the back keeping the flock moving on. David proclaimed that not only do we have Jesus as our Good Shepherd, but we have goodness and love as sheepdogs in our lives.

We may never feel like we are good enough or do enough or do well enough. We may encounter critics and attackers—enemies—in the workplace. But we can follow in Jesus' footsteps and respond with kindness. And we can look to Jesus, our Good Shepherd, and know—as King David did—the blessings of being in His flock, followed behind by goodness and mercy. Whether the workplace is an office, home, or a place where you volunteer, choose to serve in God's power and with His grace.

LIFELINE

When expectations are unrealistic and people criticize or attack, follow Jesus' example of being silent and James's wise counsel to be "quick to listen, slow to speak, and slow to become angry" (1:19).

DIGGING DEEPER

LIFELINE
When expectations are unrealistic and people criticize or attack, follow Jesus' example of being silent and James's wise counsel to be "quick to listen, slow to speak, and slow to become angry" (1:19).

"Do to others as you would have them do to you."
JESUS IN LUKE 6:31

Do not take revenge, my dear friends, but leave room for God's wrath, for it is written: "It is mine to avenge; I will repay," says the Lord.
ROMANS 12:19

It is God's will that by doing good you should silence the ignorant talk of foolish people.
1 PETER 2:15

Below, write down any ideas prompted by either these verses or the following questions...

_____
_____
_____
_____

In what ways is Jesus' command in Luke 6:31 simple but not easy? What keeps obedience from being easy?

What fuels the desire to act in revenge? Why does the Lord not want us to do that?

When have you seen—or experienced yourself—a time when "doing good" did indeed silence foolish, mean, or hostile people? In your opinion, why does kindness often have that effect?

IN REAL LIFE

Two thousand years ago the apostle James wrote, "Be doers of the word, and not hearers only" (1:22). Reading and understanding the Bible is good, but it's not enough. We also need to put into action what we read. We need to be "doers of the word."

What idea from today's reading seems to be just for you?

What will you do in response to that insight? Be specific.

TALK IT THROUGH

We tend to make prayer more complicated than it needs to be. Prayer is simply having a conversation with God: we listen, and we speak.

LIFELINE
When expectations are unrealistic and people criticize or attack, follow Jesus' example of being silent and James's wise counsel to be "quick to listen, slow to speak, and slow to become angry" (1:19).

Listening
Spend a few minutes simply being quiet. As you consider the ideas in today's reading—including the LifeLine—what thoughts does God bring to mind? You may get a sense that you are to start doing something—or stop doing something. Perhaps you will recognize some changes that might be good to make.

Talking
Speak to God as if He is sitting right next to you—and use the everyday words you would use if you were talking to a friend. Thank God for what He has taught you about dealing with hostile people not only in the workplace but wherever you encounter them. Ask Him to help you use what you've learned. One of these may help you get started:

Enable me to die to myself and to my natural desires to retaliate, seek revenge, and defend myself with words that might not be kind.

Give me the ability to share Your love with people I struggle to love.

THE WEEK IN REVIEW

Recognize burnout as the reason for distorted priorities, damaged perspective, and a derailed sense of purpose.

▶

First aid for burnout includes food, rest, and emotional venting.

▶

Focus on God, not on your problem.

▶

When dealing with hostile workers, accept that you can't live at peace with everyone; don't retaliate, and always respond with love.

▶

When expectations are unrealistic and people criticize or attack, follow Jesus' example of being silent and James's wise counsel to be "quick to listen, slow to speak, and slow to become angry."

For Personal Reflection or Group Discussion

Describe the ever-widening circle of damage, if not destruction, that workaholism can cause. What is God's counsel for preventing workaholism? for releasing us from workaholism?

Remember the statistics about how many people quit their jobs each day and how many could work harder at their jobs if they wanted to? After this week of study, what advice or encouragement would you offer someone in one or both of those positions?

What perspective could make the work you do eternally significant? See Colossians 3:23.

What impact on eternity could you have in your workplace? Be specific.

What in the workplace makes it hard for you to focus on God? What in your heart and mind makes it hard for you to focus on God?

What role does the Holy Spirit play in your responding to hostile people the way your heavenly Father wants you to?

1

MONEY

BECOMING A GIVER

The young boys were bragging on their dads. "My dad writes a few words, publishes that poem, and gets $100!"

The next boy topped that: "My dad writes a few words, publishes his new song, and makes $1,000!"

Then the preacher's kid spoke up: "My dad writes a few words, preaches his sermon, and it takes eight people to collect all the money!"

Whatever you or I get paid to do, God is the ultimate Source of our income, and He provides us with money as a tool to use in life.

> **GOD'S PLAN FOR YOU IS TO BE LIKE HIM, AND HE IS A GIVER.**

God also gives us money so we can learn to be givers. God's plan for you is to be like Him, and He is a Giver.

Whenever we give, we experience the blessing and joy of giving. Whenever we give, we are acting according to the realities of God's kingdom. So when we give, we never know what's going to happen. We're getting involved in something that's much bigger than us!

We see that in the gospel of Mark when someone's giving changed lives, solved problems, and became the focal point of a miracle.

Let's set the scene:

When Jesus landed and saw a large crowd, he had compassion on them, because they were like sheep without a shepherd. So he began teaching them many things.

By this time it was late in the day, so his disciples came to him. "This is a remote place," they said, "and it's already very late. Send the people away so they can go to the surrounding countryside and villages and buy themselves something to eat." (Mark 6:34-36)

The disciples face an obvious problem: large crowd... remote location... nothing to eat.

But what we human beings view as a problem, God regards as an opportunity for Him to do something only He can do.

Furthermore, if you don't have a problem, you don't need God to work. But God is known for solving problems. I always say, "You're going to be known either for the problems you create or the problems you solve." God is known to be a problem solver, so we can look at our problem as an open door for God to move in our lives.

Once we recognize the problem and choose to view it as an opportunity for God to work, we need to accept some responsibility for it. We need to be willing to put some skin in the game. God wants to see our genuine concern about the people impacted by the problem before He does anything about the situation.

Jesus definitely saw His disciples' concern for people in the crowd. They went to Jesus saying, "Look at all these people out here. They're hungry. What are we going to do?" They accepted responsibility.

Question: Who saw the need first, Jesus or the disciples? Who anticipated the problem, Jesus or the disciples? Jesus, of course. In fact, He knew well in advance—long before anyone else thought about it—that they were going to have a problem with food. But here's the point: Jesus did nothing about the problem until the disciples got concerned. Once they accepted responsibility, Jesus started acting. But I'm getting ahead of myself.

Notice Jesus' response when the disciples saw the need and went to Jesus wondering how they could feed 5,000+ hungry people. In Mark 6:37, Jesus said, "You give them something to eat!"

What?! Imagine facing an impossible situation and hearing Jesus say, "You do it! You are the solution." Saying this to His disciples, Jesus was getting them to accept responsibility for a problem that seemed impossible both practically and financially. The disciples had done a little cost analysis: feeding the crowd would "take more than half a year's wages" (v. 37). "Lord, we can't afford that! We don't have the money," they said. Their figures were right, but their faith was wrong.

The point is, God often asks us to do something that's impossible. Jesus said, "You feed them!" Why does He do that? Why does He ask us to do the impossible?

God wants to see what we are willing to do before He does anything. He wants to see what step of faith we will take toward resolving the problem before He steps in. God stretches and matures our faith when He asks us to do the impossible and then waits to act.

LIFELINE
When giving generously to support God's work seems impossible, take a step of faith, give anyway, and watch God work.

DIGGING DEEPER

LIFELINE
When giving generously to support God's work seems impossible, take a step of faith, give anyway, and watch God work.

Whoever sows sparingly will also reap sparingly, and whoever sows generously will also reap generously.
2 CORINTHIANS 9:6

Each of you should give what you have decided in your heart to give, not reluctantly or under compulsion, for God loves a cheerful giver.
2 CORINTHIANS 9:7

The love of money is a root of all kinds of evil. Some people, eager for money, have wandered from the faith and pierced themselves with many griefs.
1 TIMOTHY 6:10

Below, write down any ideas prompted by either these verses or the following questions...

I once heard a pastor say, "Give until it hurts. Then keep giving until it stops hurting." Discuss what he meant by the first sentence... by the second... and by stating them together.

Why does a giver's cheerfulness matter to God?

What kinds of evil can the love of money lead to? What can we do to avoid falling into the trap of loving money?

IN REAL LIFE

Two thousand years ago the apostle James wrote, "Be doers of the word, and not hearers only" (1:22). Reading and understanding the Bible is good, but it's not enough. We also need to put into action what we read. We need to be "doers of the word."

What idea from today's reading seems to be just for you?

What will you do in response to that insight? Be specific.

TALK IT THROUGH

We tend to make prayer more complicated than it needs to be. Prayer is simply having a conversation with God: we listen, and we speak.

LIFELINE
When giving generously to support God's work seems impossible, take a step of faith, give anyway, and watch God work.

Listening
Spend a few minutes simply being quiet. As you consider the ideas in today's reading—including the LifeLine—what thoughts does God bring to mind? You may get a sense that you are to start doing something—or stop doing something. Perhaps you will recognize some changes that might be good to make.

Talking
Speak to God as if He is sitting right next to you—and use the everyday words you would use if you were talking to a friend. Thank God for what He has taught you about how He wants you to use the money He entrusts to you. Ask Him to help you live according to what you've learned. One of these may help you get started:

Forgive my lack of faith and the fear that keeps me withholding money that You want me to give.

Please transform my heart, make me more generous with the money You entrust to my care and show me how I can cooperate with You in that transformation process.

2

MONEY

A BOY'S EXAMPLE

During an economic recession, two businessmen were talking. Jack said, "I'm about to lose my job, and our house is in foreclosure—but I don't worry about it."

Bob asked him, "How can you not be worried?"

"I've hired a professional worrier. He does all my worrying for me."

Bob replied, "That's a great idea. How much does it cost to hire a professional worrier?"

Jack answered, "$50,000 a year."

"$50,000! Where are you going to get that kind of money?"

Jack said, "I don't know. That's his worry!"

Oh, if only we could let other people not just worry for us, but also resolve those situations they are worrying about for us! When the disciples faced the difficult (impossible?) situation of feeding 5,000 people, though, Jesus didn't give them an out. And their three-part response to the problem—that would soon be very much theirs to solve—was a very common reaction.

First—and intentionally or not—the disciples procrastinated. When did they approach Jesus? "Late in the day" (Mark 6:35). The disciples had all day to see the potential problem, brainstorm solutions, and come up with a plan, but they didn't get around to dealing with the situation until the end of the day. Well aware of the impending crisis, Jesus nevertheless waited on His disciples to raise the issue with Him.

And when the disciples finally did approach Jesus, they were more than willing to not take any responsibility at all: "Send the people away" (v. 36).

Look the other way. Pretend the need doesn't exist. Pass the buck. The disciples were essentially saying, "It's not our problem."

Yet at the same time, the disciples' anxiety went into overdrive when Jesus said very clearly, "You give them something to eat" (v. 37). With those words ringing in their ears, they started worrying. Where would they get six months of a man's wages?

The disciples' reaction was typical: procrastinate, pass the buck, and worry. Yet Jesus, the solution to the seemingly impossible problem, was standing right there with them.

So when you need a miracle, do the opposite of what the disciples have done up to this point. Accept responsibility for the problem. Skip the procrastinating, passing the buck, and worrying. Instead, do whatever you can do with whatever you have—something the disciples did only after Jesus nudged them.

In Mark 6, the Twelve did as Jesus instructed and found five little barley loaves and two small fish. In his gospel, the apostle John gave credit to the boy who had brought a lunch and gave it to Jesus.

> **DO WHATEVER YOU CAN DO WITH WHATEVER YOU HAVE.**

We can learn from this boy who, first, gave God what he had. Of course, you can't give what you don't have, but do we choose to give what we do have? This boy had some cheap barley loaves and probably a couple of sardines. And he gave what he had.

Never underestimate what God can do through ordinary people and the limited resources that they give to Him in faith.

In fact, the boy gave God all he had, all five loaves and both fish. He didn't hold anything back from God. Notice that he didn't tithe his lunch: "Here's ten percent of this fish and half of one loaf." This boy is a role model: he gave what he had, and he gave all he had.

Finally, the boy gave his lunch willingly. He didn't hesitate, he didn't ask for time to think about it, he didn't wonder if his mom would fuss at him for not eating the lunch she had made for him. The boy simply gave.

Why don't we give the money that God has entrusted to us with the same generosity and willingness that the boy demonstrated when he gave the disciples his lunch? I think there are two reasons. First, we're worried that we might end up going hungry ourselves, that we won't have enough money to meet our needs. Second, we may think that the little we give won't make much difference, so why bother giving anything?

We give knowing God will continue to take care of us, and we give what we have—as little as it seems to us—because God can make a little go a long way. Ask one of those 5,000 people!

LIFELINE
Give willingly knowing that God will continue to provide for you and that He makes a little go a long way.

DIGGING DEEPER

LIFELINE
Give willingly knowing that God will continue to provide for you and that He makes a little go a long way.

[The 5,000+] all ate and were satisfied, and the disciples picked up twelve basketfuls of broken pieces that were left over.
LUKE 9:17

The important thing is to be willing to give as much as we can—that is what God accepts, and no one is asked to give what he has not got.
2 CORINTHIANS 8:12 PHILLIPS

Command [those who are rich] to do good, to be rich in good deeds, and to be generous and willing to share.
1 TIMOTHY 6:18

Below, write down any ideas prompted by either these verses or the following questions...

_____

_____

_____

_____

_____

After all 5,000+ were fed, the disciples picked up the leftovers. What does the existence of twelve basketfuls of leftovers tell us about God's character?

Why does not having a lot to give discourage us from giving anything at all? (Who would be the author of that idea?)

Why do we human beings need to be commanded to share willingly and generously the money God entrusts to our care?

IN REAL LIFE

Two thousand years ago the apostle James wrote, "Be doers of the word, and not hearers only" (1:22). Reading and understanding the Bible is good, but it's not enough. We also need to put into action what we read. We need to be "doers of the word."

What idea from today's reading seems to be just for you?

What will you do in response to that insight? Be specific.

TALK IT THROUGH

We tend to make prayer more complicated than it needs to be. Prayer is simply having a conversation with God: we listen, and we speak.

LIFELINE
Give willingly knowing that God will continue to provide for you and that He makes a little go a long way.

Listening
Spend a few minutes simply being quiet. As you consider the ideas in today's reading—including the LifeLine—what thoughts does God bring to mind? You may get a sense that you are to start doing something—or stop doing something. Perhaps you will recognize some changes that might be good to make.

Talking
Speak to God as if He is sitting right next to you—and use the everyday words you would use if you were talking to a friend. Thank God for what He has taught you about how He wants you to use the money He entrusts to you. Ask Him to help you use what you've learned. One of these may help you get started:

> *Lord, help me know what it means for me to give to You and to Your church "as much as I can."*

> *Please give me the gift of greater faith so that I'm able to trust You enough to generously support Your work in this world with the money You entrust to me.*

3

MONEY

IF SAVING IS A FOREIGN LANGUAGE

With a record of just 23 wins against 59 losses, the 2007 New York Knicks once again proved that money won't solve everything. While their payroll was at the top of the NBA, the Knicks on-court performance left them dead last in the Eastern Conference. In fact, their 23 wins cost the franchise over $5 million apiece.

Those were pricey wins—and what a horrible investment! It's easy to see that 2007 season as a huge waste of money. Had it been a winning season, though, people would have good reason to invest in the team. You see, giving is much more fun when we can count on an entirely positive outcome.

And when we give to God, we can with complete confidence expect God to work.

But standing before 5,000 hungry people, how confident were the disciples? Knowing both the headcount and the meager rations Jesus was working with, the disciples may have been at least a little curious and perhaps a bit expectant about what would happen next:

> *Jesus directed them to have all the people sit down in groups on the green grass. So they sat down in groups of hundreds and fifties. Taking the five loaves and the two fish and looking up to heaven, he gave thanks and broke the loaves. Then he gave them to his disciples to set before the people. He also divided the two fish among them all. They all ate and were satisfied. (Mark 6:39-42)*

We don't know how this happened. We simply know that Jesus kept breaking off pieces of bread and fish until everyone had eaten and was "satisfied."

So expect God—who specializes in doing things that are humanly impossible—to work.

And embrace the fact that you can't outgive God. Remember the twelve baskets of leftover bread and fish. Remember, too, that 5,000 refers to the number of men in the crowd, not the women and children who were also fed. Whenever you give something to God in faith, His blessing is incredible.

So what is the central lesson of this story? I think it is this truth: What we want God to do for us, He waits to do through us. His working through us requires a radical change in us. And change is painful. Most people won't find the courage to change until the pain of where they exceed the pain of making a change.

You may be one of the 70 percent of Americans who live paycheck to paycheck. If so—and for your own good, for the good of your family and your future—change that! Stop living with the pain of what-if: What if the car breaks down? What if the kids have to go to the doctor?

> **WHAT WE WANT GOD TO DO FOR US, HE WAITS TO DO THROUGH US.**

The first step toward making that change is acknowledging the problem. Did you know that 90 percent of solving a problem is realizing there is a problem? Today is your day to admit to the problem. Don't live in denial. And then take some practical steps: Keep good records. Plan your spending. Save little by little. Return 10% to God. Enjoy what you have. Cultivate contentment. Control debt. And as you undertake these important steps, know that you don't have to reinvent the wheel. Many resources are available to help you establish a budget and manage your money.

One more thing. Quit trying to keep up with the Joneses. You know, far too many of us buy things we don't need with money we don't have to impress people we don't like. This kind of peer pressure and various cultural expectations will kill you financially.

So don't even consider keeping up with the Joneses... because they're broke! They spend a lot more money than they make—and our nation has way too many Joneses. Did you know, for instance, that 49 percent of Americans could cover less than one month's expenses if they lost their income? That's not a good situation.

Spending is generally easier than saving. And spending comes easily, even naturally, to a lot of us, but saving money is like speaking a foreign language. Do what you can to learn to speak the language of saving. It's an effort you will never regret.

LIFELINE

Identify the greatest challenge you face when it comes to money management and determine—perhaps with another person's help—what you will do to meet that challenge.

DIGGING DEEPER

LIFELINE
Identify the greatest challenge you face when it comes to money management and determine—perhaps with another person's help—what you will do to meet that challenge.

Money that comes easily disappears quickly, but money that is gathered little by little will grow.
PROVERBS 13:11

"From everyone who has been given much, much will be demanded; and from the one who has been entrusted with much, much more will be asked."
JESUS IN LUKE 12:48

Keep your lives free from the love of money, and be satisfied with what you have. God has said, "I will never leave you; I will never abandon you."
HEBREWS 13:5 QUOTING DEUTERONOMY 31:6

Below, write down any ideas prompted by either these verses or the following questions...

Explain what Jesus means in Luke 12:48 as it pertains to money. What else might Jesus be referring to when He talks about the "much" people have been given?

Why does the author of Hebrews quote Deuteronomy 31:6 after he has said, "Keep your lives free from the love of money, and be satisfied with what you have"?

IN REAL LIFE

Two thousand years ago the apostle James wrote, "Be doers of the word, and not hearers only" (1:22). Reading and understanding the Bible is good, but it's not enough. We also need to put into action what we read. We need to be "doers of the word."

What idea from today's reading seems to be just for you?

What will you do in response to that insight? Be specific.

TALK IT THROUGH

We tend to make prayer more complicated than it needs to be. Prayer is simply having a conversation with God: we listen, and we speak.

LIFELINE
Identify the greatest challenge you face when it comes to money management and determine—perhaps with another person's help—what you will do to meet that challenge.

Listening
Spend a few minutes simply being quiet. As you consider the ideas in today's reading—including the LifeLine—what thoughts does God bring to mind? You may get a sense that you are to start doing something—or stop doing something. Perhaps you will recognize some changes that might be good to make.

Talking
Speak to God as if He is sitting right next to you—and use the everyday words you would use if you were talking to a friend. Thank God for what He has taught you about how He wants you to use the money He entrusts to you. Ask Him to help you use what you've learned. One of these may help you get started:

> Lord, I want a heart of contentment—and I want to work with You as You do that work of transformation.

> When you demand me to do something because of what You have blessed me with, when You ask me to do something because of what You have entrusted to me, please bless me with courage, faith, and a generous spirit.

4

MONEY

IT WILL RAIN!

When our daughter, Haley, was thirteen years old, she started using the Envelope System to manage her money. One day when I looked at her envelopes, I saw that they were labeled "Emergency," "Crafting," "Trips," "Gas Money," and "Christmas."

I was impressed that, at thirteen, she was already saving for gas for a car! Then, curious, I asked her about her envelope labeled "Emergency." "Haley, what kind of emergency are you saving for?"

She said, "Dad, I don't know! That's why they call it an emergency!"

Again, I was impressed. At thirteen, Haley understood that she—and you and I, too—will encounter financial emergencies and unexpected expenses. The car will need a new transmission. A parent's failing health will necessitate an unforeseen airplane flight. The landlord will increase the rent, or the house you own will need a new roof. To experience the financial security of saving, you must remember that rainstorms like these happen.

> "A SENSIBLE MAN WATCHES FOR PROBLEMS AHEAD AND PREPARES TO MEET THEM."

And, as Solomon wrote in Proverbs 27:12, "A sensible man watches for problems ahead and prepares to meet them. The simple-minded never looks and suffers the consequences" (TLB).

The sensible move is to prepare for the problems you will encounter. Even though you don't know what those problems will be, you need to be ready to address them. That means you need a rainy day fund. You need an umbrella. You need an emergency fund. And that emergency fund is not for buying things or for going on vacation; it is for emergencies only.

That emergency fund is for those time when Murphy's Law—"If it can go wrong, it will"—strikes. You may already think Murphy is a member of your family. But understand something: if you will start being a wise manager of money, Murphy leaves. In fact, saving money for emergencies is Murphy repellent, and being broke all the time seems to attract him.

Most of America says, "Well if an emergency arises, I'll just use a credit card." That only works if you pay off your credit card bill every month, and if that credit card is used for an emergency, you'll only be able to pay it off if you have an emergency fund. Other pseudo-savers consider non-emergencies like Christmas reason enough to dip into the emergency fund. Christmas is not an emergency; it doesn't sneak up on you. Christmas has always been in December and will always be in December. You can expect it and plan for it, so Christmas is not an emergency. Similarly, your car will need repairs, and the kids will outgrow their clothes. These are not emergencies; they are items that belong in your budget. If you don't budget for them, though, they will feel like emergencies.

I hope you're convinced that you need to start saving, that you need to establish that emergency fund. So let me tell you how to save $1,000 in cash fast. If you have a household income under $20,000 per year, use $500 to start your rainy day fund. Those who earn more than $20,000 should get together $1,000 fast to start your rainy day fund.

You should start here. Don't reduce your debt first. Build an emergency fund first because emergencies will kill your debt-reducing plan faster than anything. If you don't have a rainy day fund and an emergency arises, you will feel forced to use that credit card, and you might feel like a failure. So start with a little fund to catch the little things before you begin getting rid of your debt. This beginning of an emergency fund will keep life's little Murphy's from turning into new debt.

You have to break the cycle—and you can!

To start that fund, first, look at your budget and see where you can cut. Skip Starbucks for a week and movies for a month. Don't buy new clothes until you establish that rainy day fund.

Work extra hours or take on another job temporarily. Deliver pizzas, work retail part-time or chauffeur kids to afterschool activities. Sell something.

Think as creatively as possible.

Then, when you get to your goal of $500 or $1,000, hide it. Put the money someplace that isn't easy for you to access. You will impulse-buy something if the money is easily accessible.

My premise is simple: If you have the financial security of an emergency fund, then you will have the freedom to experience the reward of giving.

LIFELINE

Establish a rainy day fund—and use it only for real emergencies.

DIGGING DEEPER

LIFELINE
Establish a rainy day fund—and use it only for real emergencies.

A sensible man watches for problems ahead and prepares to meet them. The simple-minded never looks and suffers the consequences.
PROVERBS 27:12 TLB

"Be on your guard against all kinds of greed; life does not consist in an abundance of possessions."
JESUS IN LUKE 12:15

"Sell your possessions and give to the poor. Provide purses for yourselves that will not wear out, a treasure in heaven that will never fail, where no thief comes near and no moth destroys. For where your treasure is, there your heart will be also."
JESUS IN LUKE 12:33-34

Below, write down any ideas prompted by either these verses or the following questions...

_____
_____
_____
_____
_____

When has a rainy day fund helped you or someone you know—and/or the absence of a rainy day fund been a problem for you or someone you know? Do you have a rainy day fund now? Why or why not?

What are some kinds of greed? And what does life consist of if not "an abundance of possessions"?

What are some ways God's people can establish "a treasure in heaven"? Be sure to address the way money can be used toward that end.

IN REAL LIFE

Two thousand years ago the apostle James wrote, "Be doers of the word, and not hearers only" (1:22). Reading and understanding the Bible is good, but it's not enough. We also need to put into action what we read. We need to be "doers of the word."

What idea from today's reading seems to be just for you?

What will you do in response to that insight? Be specific.

TALK IT THROUGH

We tend to make prayer more complicated than it needs to be. Prayer is simply having a conversation with God: we listen, and we speak.

LIFELINE
Establish a rainy day fund—and use it only for real emergencies.

Listening
Spend a few minutes simply being quiet. As you consider the ideas in today's reading—including the LifeLine—what thoughts does God bring to mind? You may get a sense that you are to start doing something—or stop doing something. Perhaps you will recognize some changes that might be good to make.

Talking
Speak to God as if He is sitting right next to you—and use the everyday words you would use if you were talking to a friend. Thank God for what He has taught you about how He wants you to use the money He entrusts to you. Ask Him to help you use what you've learned. One of these may help you get started:

> *Purify my heart so that I may desire, invest in, and store up treasure in heaven.*

> *You taught, Lord Jesus, life is not about material possessions. Free me from the attraction of all the world offers and all the culture says I need.*

5

MONEY

HONORING GOD BY OUR GIVING

When it comes to giving, if you won't give a dime out of a dollar, you won't give $1 million out of $10 million.

This truth changed my life.

My wife, Terri, and I know that God will hold us accountable for how we use what He provides for us. We know we are to hold what God has entrusted to us with an open hand, not a closed fist. In other words, we must always be ready and willing to give when God directs us to because, after all, He has given us everything we have. What we have is His, and we are to remember that.

Since adopting this attitude and approach to giving, Terri and I have learned that it is impossible to outgive God: whenever we are faithful to give, He is faithful to provide.

And—as I mentioned—we also know that giving and tithing starts with that first dime out of every dollar. Believe me when I say that this kind of giving is possibly the most fun you will ever have with your money. Giving is also a source of profound joy. Consider the sacrificial giving of Jesus' friend Mary when He visited her, her sister, and her brother in Bethany.

While Jesus was sitting at a table with His disciples, Mary entered the room, knelt at His feet, broke open her alabaster box, and poured its contents onto His feet. She then wiped His feet with her hair. The fragrance of the perfume filled the air… and so did the tension.

Judas was quick to try to put Mary in her place: "What a waste of money! We could have fed the poor!" But Jesus honored Mary for her offering that honored Him. Below are four qualities of an offering that honors God.

We give something that is important to us.

Mary did exactly that when she "took a pound of very costly oil" to anoint Jesus' feet with (John 12:3 NKJV).

> JESUS HONORED MARY FOR HER OFFERING THAT HONORED HIM.

God is not honored by token gifts, by our dipping a finger into our own alabaster box and dabbing a little on Him. Mary's oil was worth 300 denarii, and one denarius was a day's wage in the first-century world. What Mary poured onto Jesus' feet was worth one year's salary.

Is the offering you give costly to you? Or is your offering just a token…a tip to God?

We give to impact someone's life.

As Mary poured out the perfume, "the house was filled with the fragrance of the oil" (v. 3).

The fragrance of her offering impacted everyone who was present. They couldn't overlook Mary's act of extravagant love, and many may have felt convicted about their lack of love. We impact people's lives when we give an offering that honors God.

When we give something important to us… that impacts someone's life… be ready to respond when people ask why.

Ironically, not everyone is excited when someone gives generously. In fact, a God-honoring offering can expose the phoniness of some people's commitment to God.

In this case, Judas spoke up: "Why was this fragrant oil not sold?" (v. 5). Implying that Mary's offering was a waste, he said that the money from the sale could have been given to the poor—and doesn't that sound spiritual?

But Mary's perfume was not for sale; it was forgiving.

Whenever we give an offering, God will understand our motives and know our hearts.

When Judas questioned Mary's action, Jesus quickly told him to "let her alone" (v. 7). Matthew reported that Jesus also said, "She has done a good work for Me'" (Matthew 26:10 NKJV).

As far as we know, no one else defended Mary's action. But the One who did was the only One whose opinion mattered: Jesus was pleased with Mary's gift, and He commended her for that "good work." Whenever we give to God something that is precious to us, He is pleased.

Jesus wrote Mary's biography that day. She never said a word, but her actions spoke volumes about the person she was. Similarly, what we do with our money tells the story of our lives. Our tithes and our offerings write our biography.

And tithing is giving 10% of what you make back to God. If that's new to you, I encourage you to try it for forty days and see what God does. Give God an opportunity to bless you with both a stronger faith and genuine joy as you learn to give more generously.

LIFELINE
Honor God by obediently and in faith supporting His kingdom work with your tithes and offerings.

DIGGING DEEPER

LIFELINE
Honor God by obediently and in faith supporting His kingdom work with your tithes and offerings.

"I desire mercy, not sacrifice, and acknowledgment of God rather than burnt offerings."
GOD IN HOSEA 6:6

"Will a mere mortal rob God? Yet you rob me.
"But you ask, 'How are we robbing you?'
"In tithes and offerings."
GOD IN MALACHI 3:8

A poor widow came and put in two very small copper coins, worth only a few cents. Calling his disciples to him, Jesus said, "Truly I tell you, this poor widow has put more into the treasury than all the others."
MARK 12:42-43

Below, write down any ideas prompted by either these verses or the following questions...

_____
_____
_____
_____
_____

What does Hosea 6:6 reveal about God's economy and what He values most?

Do you think the word robbing in Malachi 3:8 is appropriate? Why or why not?

Why is less, more in Mark 12:42–43? What is God saying to you, instructing you, or convicting you about in these two verses? Be specific about His message to you and what you will do in response.

IN REAL LIFE

Two thousand years ago the apostle James wrote, "Be doers of the word, and not hearers only" (1:22). Reading and understanding the Bible is good, but it's not enough. We also need to put into action what we read. We need to be "doers of the word."

What idea from today's reading seems to be just for you?

What will you do in response to that insight? Be specific.

TALK IT THROUGH

We tend to make prayer more complicated than it needs to be. Prayer is simply having a conversation with God: we listen, and we speak.

LIFELINE
Honor God by obediently and in faith supporting His kingdom work with your tithes and offerings.

Listening
Spend a few minutes simply being quiet. As you consider the ideas in today's reading—including the LifeLine—what thoughts does God bring to mind? You may get a sense that you are to start doing something—or stop doing something. Perhaps you will recognize some changes that might be good to make.

Talking
Speak to God as if He is sitting right next to you—and use the everyday words you would use if you were talking to a friend. Thank God for what He has taught you about how He wants you to use the money He entrusts to you. Ask Him to help you use what you've learned. One of these may help you get started:

> *Please give me a pure, generous, and trusting heart like the widow Jesus saw in the temple clearly had.*

> *Show me where I am robbing You of the tithes and offerings of not just my treasure, but of my time and talents as well.*

THE WEEK IN REVIEW

⟵ LIFELINES ⟶
for Money

When giving more money to support God's work seems impossible, take a step of faith, give anyway, and watch God work.

▶

Give willingly knowing that God will continue to provide for you and that He makes a little go a long way.

▶

Identify the greatest challenge you face when it comes to money management and determine— perhaps with another person's help—what you will do to meet that challenge.

▶

Establish a rainy day fund—and use it only for real emergencies.

▶

Honor God by obediently and in faith by supporting His kingdom work with your tithes and offerings.

For Personal Reflection or Group Discussion

What incentive to give "your" money freely and generously do you find in the truth that all that you have is God's in the first place?

Why do worrying and money seem to go together?

Jesus calls us to have a childlike faith. What do we learn about childlike faith from the boy who had five barley loaves and two sardines?

What is the value of having a rainy day fund? of saving money? Why is establishing these funds/habits difficult for you—and what might make it easier? Or, if keeping a rainy day fund and faithfully saving is easy for you, why do you think that's the case?

What does it mean that you can't outgive God? Why is this truth an important context for a discussion about money, tithes, and offerings?

What we do with our money tells the story of our lives. Offer an overview of your bio up to this point. Think, too, about what you would like to have happen in the next chapter of your life story as well as in the story's closing pages—and what you will do to make that happen.